AF407733

Life Coaching That Works

Charles Sanderfur

Copy Rights © 2023 by Charles Sanderfur

All Rights Reserved

No part of this publication may be reproduced, distributed, or transmitted in any form or by any means, including photocopying, recording, or other electronic or mechanical methods, without the prior written permission of the publisher, except in the case of brief quotations embodied in critical reviews and certain other non-commercial uses permitted by copyright law.

Published in the United States by Charles Sanderfur

Dedication

I dedicate this to the one person who each day, amazes me with her ability to love far beyond human capacity; the person who for over has undergirded me during my greatest victories, and wept, cuddled, and encouraged me in my most disgraced failures. If ever 1 allow myself an ounce of consideration toward giving up on our dream, I only imagined her sweet reassuring face and my self-pity was immediately interrupted with emotions of drive and determination.

In a noble attempt to relinquish to women, their rightful, innate, and earned equal place in society, I am concerned that the most important and influential role of women has unfortunately, been downgraded. Women, who are good in this role, are often considered problematic for the fight against inequality; even though equality has always been innately theirs.

I dedicate this to the one person who, while educating herself and working for more than twenty years outside home; insisted on investing the quality time necessary to mother and raise 3 biological and 6 adopted, absolutely amazing children—all of whom now greatly contribute to society. While I have met and admired hundreds of great people, I have only one true hero: my darling wife,

Marlene.

I dedicate this book to you, sweetie; the greatest coach I ever had.

Special Thanks

My very special thanks to Cindy and Ethan Sanderfur, Lee Sultan, Rick, and Karen Thompson and Nancy Willis for all your assistance in the production of this book.

About the Author

Charles Sanderfur is a National Board-Certified Life and Executive Coach, with the Center for Credentialing and Education, a Nationally Certified Psychotherapist and holds Ordination Credentials with the Assemblies of God U.S.A. He received graduate training at the University of Tennessee, and coaching certification and training at the Institute of Life Coach Training and the College of Executive Coaching Pismo Beach, California.

He is best known for his work with ordinary people, assisting them to reach success levels often beyond their own current dreams.

Great numbers of clients attribute to Dr. Sanderfur the credit for helping them to first believe in themselves, then plan their life path and ultimately achieve great success. He has been the coach behind great educational, business, and life achievements by individuals by drawing out the greatness already there but lying dormant.

For the past 37 years he has served as Lead Pastor for New Vision Church of Knoxville, Tennessee and done extensive work with Foster and Adoptive children through the Patria Foster Care Agency and Koinonia Counseling Center. Dr. Sanderfur is clearly a practitioner who has written this book for practitioners to be able to quickly apply the effective techniques of Solution Focused

Life Coaching.

A firm believer in the words of emancipator Fredrick Douglas who said, *"It's easier to build strong children than to repair broken men;"* Dr. Sanderfur makes time to coach children and teens challenging them to play the music that has been placed within them; to dream large and to chase their dreams.

Married for 48 years to his college sweetheart Marlene; they have 3 biological, six adopted and 11 grandchildren.

A former college athlete, he has worked with legends in the sports and entertainment fields including the late great Gospel Singer Jessy Dixon and NFL hall of fame Defensive End Reggie White. A powerful motivational speaker and writer he makes special effort to fill public speaking requests in order to reach numbers of people with his inspiring message of "arising each morning to chase one's dream every day."

Dr. Sanderfur has for the greater part of his life been driven by the words of George Bernard Shaw,

"Some men see things as they are and ask why, but I dream, dreams that never were and ask why not?"

He can be contacted at: motivation4lifecoach.com.

Table of Contents

Foreword...i

Preface iv

Introduction 1

General Coaching Guidelines and Objectives 5

Chapter 1..6

Believe in Yourself...

Chapter 2...14

Organized Chit Chat..

Chapter 3...24

Selecting from the 'Cream Rising to the Top' ....

Chapter 4...41

Visualization: Helping clients to see themselves living it.

Chapter 5...50

Establishing Winning Strategies,.................................

Chapter 6...57

Communication: It's your best Tool ....

Chapter 7...67

The Solution Focused Coaching Process ....

Chapter 8...74

Why Solution Focused Coaching Works..........................

Chapter 9 87

Now, Just Do it ....

Conclusion 98

Definitions, Designations and Descriptions 101

References 105

Endnotes 107

Foreword

I've known Dr. Sanderfur for the past 24 years, both professionally and as a personal friend. He certainly possesses natural life coaching skills to undergird his extensive education and training in psychotherapy, life coaching and ministry. In this, his latest book *Life Coaching That Works,* he gives us a refreshing approach to life coaching that reminds me of why I have been successful as a professional athlete and minister during my life.

These concepts are excellent and promote much of what I have learned over the years related to dedication, determination, discipline, and accountability.

I have witnessed firsthand the influence

Dr. Sanderfur has had in the lives of many people; motivating numbers of kids, teens, and adults to *"live their greatest dreams."* This has been done through coaching them into making the preparations necessary to finish educational goals, obtain promotions, start lucrative businesses and work effectively in ministry and with community agencies.

What I see in *Solution Focused Coaching Simplified* is an easy to apply, transferable model *that has worked*. **It is** what Dr. Sanderfur has been doing throughout his career with many people.

Within this book are many techniques, phrases, ideas, and powerful questions I often heard during the times we worked together. What makes these ideas so efficient is the congruence he maintains with life, and profession. It would be difficult to count the numbers of adults and children whose lives are changed, and futures given enormous positivity through the influence of Dr. Sanderfur as a Life Coach, Therapist and Minister.

My recommendation would be to read the entire book for training and inspiration, then refer back often, and you will discover great answers among the powerful questions associated with Life Coaching. You will appreciate relevant words of athletic coaches and enjoy examples of friends and professional colleagues, helping you to grow as a life coach and an individual.

Art Moore

Art Moore was a powerful defensive end with the New England Patriots and San Francisco 49ers during the 1970's. Dr. Sanderfur worked with Art and his wife Gail, Contemporary Gospel Music Artist, to start Yes I Can Ministry, now a tremendously successful program serving our nations at-risk youth. They may be contacted at www.YesICan1.com.

Preface

Good Coaching Brings Out The Best In People.

Coaching uses powerful and insightful questions to surface deeply concealed dreams, potential and life development goals; then uses more questions to hold the owner of those goals responsible for creating strategies, to seize their greatest dreams.

It seems silly to think Stephen Curry, Tiger Woods, and Tom Brady for all of their careers continued to insist upon more and more coaching, unless you clearly understand that *"only coaching can excavate deeply concealed greatness," in sports and in life."*

What is Solution Focused Coaching ?

Solution Focused Coaching is rooted in the solution focused therapy approach. The Solution Focused Brief Therapy (SFBT) approach has enjoyed great success with clients and is appreciated for its brief approach involving little attention to problems and strong emphasis on solutions. The concepts and processes involved in SFBT were developed by, Steve de Shazer and Insoo Kim Berg a husband and wife team and those working at The Brief Family Therapy Center in Milwaukee, Wisconsin[i].

Solution Focused Coaches, like Solution Focused

Therapist, seek to help clients identify skills, resources, strengths, and other qualities already possessed by the client which can be tapped and used to reach the goals which are set. Coaches empower clients through powerful probing questions like The Miracle Question, scaling questions, pinpointing problem exceptions and other Solution Focused coaching techniques to facilitate the best opportunity for change and achievement.

I believe the success of Solution Focused Coaching is directly attributed to the fact that Solution Focused Therapy of all other approaches more closely resembles the dynamics of what makes coaching successful; powerful solution excavating questions. The following chapters contain instructions on the application of solution focused coaching, while continuing to give deeper definition to this approach.

You will appreciate the simplicity not only of Solution Focused Coaching but of this book's writing style as well. When life coaches try and mimic the at times boring, and often condescending snobbery existing in some academic fields, we lose an edge. I've read too many books to number the times when I have encountered this attitude. As a result, I am a sponge for information regardless of the writing style.

However I must confess that people like Tony Robbins, Dennis Waitley, Zig Ziglar, and Brian Tracy make the reading much more than the drabness of a student thesis or dissertation often totally absent of humanness, humor, and practicality. Ralph Waldo

Emerson said, "Nothing great was ever achieved without enthusiasm[ii].

As a former college athlete, coach, minister, and therapist, I have learned that to intertwine life experience with the wisdom of people who may have never written anything is not only invaluable, but it also makes learning much more pleasurable.

I am not sure if Yogi Berra could spell empirical or dissertation, but he sure knew a lot about getting the best out of people through coaching. Yogi once said

"In theory there is no difference between theory and practice. In practice there is."

He also said,

"If you don't know where you are going, you might wind up somewhere else."[iii]

Some of the people who have molded my life the most have been mentors, teachers, athletic coaches, ministers, relatives, and friends.

As I think back on how they contributed to my success it was done in various ways. At times they taught and modeled; and at other times they lectured and trained. But as I now recall there were certain times when each of them would spend time doing what we have now come to call life coaching. They were life coaching when life coaching wasn't cool.

Even my mother who only finished the 12th grade

would call me by my childhood name and say, "Now CW what are you going to do about that?" Or "Can you figure out a way that you could do that a little better?" And my mind would race 90 mph trying to come up with solutions to solve the problem or do a better job. Of course this would come after much training from both parents to never do anything in mediocrity, to always give your best effort and to do everything with excellence.

We don't have a record of who, but someone once said,

> *"If a task is once begun never leave it until it is done, Be the labor great or small do it well or not at all."*

Because I was the beneficiary of life coaching from great coaches who had no clue as to what they were doing, I refuse to offer to the public something that has no appeal or little benefit to those who may or may not ever even consider graduate studies.

You can help clients to achieve their greatest dreams using the simplicity of life coaching through insight, active listening, and solution focused power questioning, if you refuse to be intimidated by the often-stagnating misuse of academia. Solution focused coaching relies heavily on what the client is doing *that is already working* and strategize to do more of exactly that. So it is important for the coach to help the client to discover times, or exceptions to certain realities.

I hope that my approach to teaching and learning will

cause the principles and strategies of solution focused life coaching to be easily understood and quickly adapted to your life coaching practice. Now, let's get this puppy off the ground! The Sky is the limit!

Introduction

"Coaching is making men (women) do what they want (to do) so they can become what they want to become."

-Tom Landry, former Dallas Cowboy Coach.

Yes, I am a lifetime Dallas Cowboy fan. I grew up in Texas and have seen happier NFL Days. When I decided to write this book on Life coaching, I chose to draw from the quotes of several athletic coaches to support some of the points I would be making. Well of course I absolutely had to start with my favorite Professional football coach, Tom Landry.

Coach Landry was a winner who did it right. He was a great coach and an even greater human being. Though his definition of coaching is somewhat dated relating to gender and slightly off relating to the power of the coach to persuade, it is still generally precisely what a life coach should endeavor to achieve.

We are not able to make anyone do anything, yet we use powerful questions to draw out of clients the plan, desire, and effort to chase their life dreams and personal goals. Every person is endowed with the seeds of greatness related to some area, skill, or talent.

A life coach may not have great knowledge as to how to perform whatever that skill may be. However the coach does know how to ask questions that will cause clients to search within themselves to discover and apply the steps necessary to become what it is they really want to become or to do what it is they really want to do in this life.

I have assisted through life skills coaching in helping people start a businesses, attend college, finish grad school, start exciting new careers and chase what was once only a distant dream. I have worked with professional athletes and entertainers such as the late Reggie White, one of the greatest NFL Defensive Ends ever and Jessy Dixon, the great Gospel singer.

This Book is designed to help life coaches apply my chosen use of Solution Focused Coaching. I have attempted to offer the most important parts of the life coaching skills in order to assist those who really want to get to work on this skill and to do so without delay.

I have known several people who by nature are great life coaches without any formal training at all. Somehow at the end of every casual conversation I have with these people about my life or career, I end up with a number of steps to make things much better; and they work! That was not the intent of the conversation, and I was not charged a fee. But it does convince me that like anything else, Life Coaching can become overly commercialized and strategized causing the practice of it to be more elusive than it really should be.

Like most other things the best coaches will be those who practice more than they read. Of course studying is essential, but it is the *practice* that develops excellent coaching. To quote the legendary Vince Lombardi, "Perfect practice makes perfect." It is my goal to get you into the practice of life coaching as quickly as possible. Solution Focus is a very simple and practical method of coaching; with understanding and practice you will quickly be able to help people reach their greatest dreams.

I had the privilege of working with the Greatest Defensive end to ever play in the NFL, the late Reggie White. For a couple of years I worked with Reggie helping him to raise awareness and funding for his Maternity Home.

I recall once when Reggie and I were speaking to a group of business professionals and clergy inviting their participation with his program. I spoke first and then Reggie got up to speak. Reggie was a drum major for morality and righteous living and when something was bothering him in society, he often zeroed in on it no matter what the purpose or setting at the time. Well Reggie literally preached a fire and brimstone sermon and hurled verbal missiles of conviction toward each and every one attending.

Afterward, he insisted upon my honest response. I asked him two good coaching questions. I asked, "What do you think they felt while you spoke?" He said, "They were pretty upset". I then said can you name the expectations we came here with? Obviously, we came to gain support for a cause that was dear to both Reggie and me. Instead, we left with a large fence mending project!

There are a number of subjects that we may pursue related to Life Coaching. It is not my desire to chase rabbits, pad this book, talk about side interests, or even mention anything that is not absolutely necessary for the purpose of getting you to begin to practice Solution Focused Coaching almost immediately.

This book is designed to help a caring person who desires to help people succeed in life and teach them quickly to do so. Our goal is to accomplish this without the reader feeling an overwhelming, overpowering push to almost become a therapist before being able to succeed as a life coach.

If you are a natural motivator; and gravitate towards facilitating strategies when faced with life's challenges; and are already performing life coaching techniques, you will benefit from this book's more focused approach.

It is important that we start with some idea of what coaching is and what it is not. This is in no way an exhaustive list of what a coach needs to know prior to working with clients. I do believe however that one can work with clients and help them greatly without studying coaching for two or three years. This book will assist a coach to use a *solution-focused* approach to coaching almost immediately, if you understand Life coaching at all. For certified coaches, this is a simple method that will lead to great results in your coaching practice while maintaining simplicity.

General Coaching Guidelines and Objectives

As a coach you are not the expert, the client is always the expert. Your primary function is to listen 80% of the time and speak 20% of the time; and of that 20%, to offer powerful thought and strategy-provoking questions related to the client's coaching focal points.

Your goal is to *empower* the client through support, compliments, acknowledgements, and endorsements.

You are **not** a counselor, therapist, or mentor; you are a coach. Probe, listen, support, and facilitate the client's strategy selections and pursuits.

As a coach, you will, through powerful questions, facilitate:

Client self-awareness

Client and or Team development

Improved skills and performance

The revealing, identifying and the chasing of your client's dreams, goals, and desires

Life, career, and relationship development

Chapter 1
Believe in Yourself

"If your dream ain't bigger than you, there is a problem with your dream."

- Deon Sanders, Head Coach, Colorado University

To paraphrase Chief Justice Oliver Wendell Holmes, the Great American Tragedy is for anyone to go to their grave with their music still in them.

Chapter Focus

This is the foundation for everything in this book. The techniques offered to you for coaching yourself and others are client-proven to be effective. The following chapters provide loads of information that will bring tremendous results to you and those you coach, all hinging on the importance of believing in yourself. The Little Engine That Could achieved what no one believed possible by constantly repeating, "I think I can, I think I can, I think I can." I want you to modify those words and use them every day of your life.

Four of the most powerful coaching words you can ever speak are, "I know I can. I know I can." They are only surpassed by the two simple words, "I will."

If you feel stuck in a job or a profession that does not offer you fulfillment, that does not define who you are. I worked in a slaughterhouse, a foundry, a chicken processing plant, and several dead-end jobs. But not a day went by that I was not dreaming of when I would complete college and graduate school and do exactly what I am doing today: living my dream!

You must allow yourself to feel the fear that attacks us all. Then do what you're destined to do anyway, despite that fear. It is absolutely fine to dream in your sleep at night. Everyone does that. But the high-level achievers wake up and live their dreams every day.

If you feel stuck like you are heading nowhere, choose today to get unstuck. Life is tough on us all. We crave relief. So, we lose ourselves in the lives of others through television, social media, and gaming. Anything more interesting to us than what is happening in our own life. We welcome the interruption. But if not corralled, those distractions are lethal, destroying your hopes and killing your dreams.

Ninety percent of the population procrastinates regularly. A Northwestern Mutual Study found that over seventy percent of America's population prefers playing it safe. The difference between that group and those who succeed in reaching their dreams is not talent or resources. It is effort!

Effort has a short life span if you don't adopt tools that motivate you to overcome the temptation to procrastinate.

You are born for success and achievement, but without a clear blueprint, you are meandering through life, and your ideas have nothing to latch onto. They come and go like clouds in the sky. You have to grab your dreams and squeeze them as if they are a vital source of life. Because they are!

Hold on to your dreams. Follow them until you arrive at your God-ordained destination, just like the box cars of a train, locked together for the distance, connected to a powerful locomotive pulling them to their destiny.

Here are five essential steps to create an unbreakable connection to your dreams, helping you reach them one by one.

Clarification

Decide what dreams you are going to chase. Be specific in choosing what you want to pursue first.

There are two questions I often use in my coaching practice as a quick way to help someone discover what their real interests are, "If you could do anything in life and get paid well for it, what would that be?" And, "If money was not an issue, what would you do with your life?"

Visualization

Always imagine yourself doing what you have chosen as your dream or life's goal. When you tell a child that they are going to Disney World in a couple of weeks, visualization immediately sets in. They vicariously visit Disney World until they finally arrive. Even at the last moment, when nearly approaching the gate, that child exhibits excitement.

To get unstuck, you must maintain an image of yourself doing what you are gifted to do. Spend tons of time dreaming about what it will be like when you are living your dream!

Contemplation

Now, this is where you establish the road map to your success. This is the planning stage. Life coaching is successful because the coach facilitates for the client to create their own steps to success. As a coach, I never develop plans for a client. The client has to do that. Your success in getting unstuck will only happen when you create detailed plans for each step leading to your goals.

A good way to do this is to start with what it looks like to have achieved the goal. Then, write down what would have to happen immediately before that. And what occurred just before that. Continue this backward examination of what comes before the next step until you get to where you are now – in this moment.

What you wrote just above that one is your first step to take in chasing your dream. And the one above that is the next step, and so on.

The first three steps of clarification, visualization, and contemplation will create a closer relationship with you and your dreams. They are designed to reaffirm your connection with and ownership of your dreams. Ownership is empowerment. No one remains stuck while unleashing empowerment.

The two remaining steps are action steps. And the universe only rewards action.

Application

One of the most unused tools to destroy procrastination is attached to a study that found that 80% of those who start any previously avoided task will continue. Just getting started begins a process in the brain that can destroy procrastination.

Continuation

Continuation depends upon a simple decision: a decision to maintain discipline. That is, doing what you are supposed to do, when you are supposed to do it, whether you feel like it or not.

There is no getting around it. You will reap what you sow. Again, the universe only rewards action. It does not reward thoughts, good intentions, or even the best plans. It only rewards action.

The person coaching themselves must ask the same question posed to a coaching client, "How bad do you want what you want?"

As a kid in San Antonio, Texas, I saw a slice of bread moving along the ground as if it were floating. Moving closer, I noticed that a group of Texas Red Ants had surrounded the slice of bread and were ever-so-slowly moving it toward their home: a hole in the ground beneath a mound of dirt. No matter how long it took, they were taking the bread to their colony.

The life coach coaching themselves or others must have the same character traits as those ants - Direction, Drive, Determination, and Discipline.

Hold yourself responsible for the directions provided by the road map you have created to reach your greatest dreams. Remain driven toward achievement - drive is the force used to get where you are destined to go. Determination is the foundational quality of those who never give up. And discipline is a decision you must make every day, at times, moment by moment. Again discipline is doing what you are supposed to do, when you are supposed to do it, whether you feel like it or not.

Your success as a life coach and in coaching yourself to greatness depends on how well you adopt these traits. They are the lifestyle habits of a winner!

And remember, you always have a choice, even related to the fear of failure that will inevitably come. You can make it an asset by remembering it is not what happens in life, it is how you take it.

My Constant Companions

I am not surprised to see you here,
My constant companions; failure, and fear.
Again I have caved, for less than what I should've
Closer to my grave, still filled with what I could've.

Failure and fear, I see you're still here.
From my innermost parts, summoned to appear
My quest to destroy you, I could never win,
Your conception, your existence, I create within.

It's Scary should I do,
It's Frightening if I don't.
It's my choice if I will,
It's my choice if I won't.

So let it be clear to both failure and fear,
I'm living my dreams now; You'll always be here.

Chapter 2
Organized Chit Chat

"Look for your choices, pick the best one, then go with it."

-Pat Riley

Pat Riley won three straight NBA championships as coach of the Los Angeles Lakers and two more with the Miami Heat as General Manager. He is one of the competent motivators of our nation.

Chapter Focus

The goal of this chapter is to impress upon the life coach the need to *learn to listen well and with purpose.* Please use this chapter to learn some listening techniques and to be motivated to research other communication skills. After putting into practice the skills taught here you should be able to identify the most important goals, dreams, and interests of your client and to agree upon the most important areas to be coached, referred to as the **Coaching Focal Points**. (CFP)

Power Question: *(Related to career, relationships, success etc.) If money, time, and ability were not obstacles, what would be your greatest dream in life?*

Many trainers of Life Coaches are adamant on insuring that the trainees grasp the difference between coaches and therapists. That is not of great concern for my purposes, however I would acknowledge that the differences are well documented and need to be understood. For our purposes there is at least one commonality; and I will point it out as it must be fully understood in order to become an effective life coach. Every coach has to master the skill of listening in order to move into the more helpful stages of life coaching.

Carl Rogers, the father of Person-Centered Therapy believed that many therapy clients could solve their own clinical issues simply by talking about them. In his very successful approach, Rogers taught students to become active listeners and develop unconditional positive regard for clients.

The success of this approach depended upon a client's internal ability to arrive at solutions to problems and disorders through the dynamics of cognitive, deductive processes. Rogers believed that this process was inevitable when humans are prompted to discuss at length their issues. The more skilled the therapist is in facilitating an atmosphere conducive to the client's continued focused speaking, the more likelihood of therapeutic success.

Similarly, in the beginning sessions, good listening skills create congruence, trust, and educates the coach as to what makes the client "tick" and what will likely be the sequence of the coaching focal points. For the coach the goal is twofold. In the early stages of the coaching relationship the coach uses active listening to hone in on and agree upon areas of coaching to be pursued or the **Coaching Focal Points**.

In the best coaching relationship the coach will only talk about 20% of the time and the client will talk about 80% of the time. This is something that every coach can use as a barometer to determine if he or she is coaching or just giving advice. Active listening takes on the appearance of organized 'chit-chat' and requires certain skills and relational factors to be effective.

The Solution Focused Life Coach always demonstrates unconditional positive regard for the client.

Listening well is a skill that will win friendships, engender endearments, and earn great respect in any field. It is simply a fact of life that those who listen more than talk are greatly appreciated in society. As a trained therapist, I recall the first time I participated in a role-play in "Introduction to Counseling" the first counseling class I ever took. I had no training in counseling at that point. Yet when my role-play partner reported to the class her experience as the counselee, she said "if ever I need counseling I'm going to Charles, I've never met anyone so easy to talk to." At that point I had no clue what I was obviously doing right. This was in 1981; I have since learned that I naturally, mentally move into the interspaces of people when I listen. Because of this I use physical and verbal cues that tell the person I am really interested, not in hurry, and deeply thinking about what they are saying. In other words, I am among those who **actively listen naturally**. It comes out of an unconditional positive regard for nearly everyone I meet.

The truth is until a person does me or someone else, I love, harm or is recognized as a menace to society, I like almost everyone I meet. I can't make the Will Roger's claim when he said, *"I never met a man I didn't like"*. That is certainly not true; I have met people I did not like at all. But it usually takes some strong effort on their part to move me to that place.

Borrowing from William Glasser's Reality Therapy, when clients feel a sense of love and belonging facilitated by the coach, great communication possibilities are born.

It is this level of communication upon which Solution Focused Life Coaching strongly depends. When a coach is able to engender this level of relationship and communication, the discovery and agreement of Coaching Focal Points are the result that follows nearly 100% of the time and so is the likelihood of coaching success.

Because much of Life Coaching is done by phone it is all the more important that the verbal communications attest to the coaches unconditional positive regard for the client. This skill must be developed and used while maintaining the 80%/20% client/coach speaking ratio. Coaching leads such as reflective listening and periodically restating the client's last phrase the coach is staying with the client. Combine this with a warm accepting voice tone and positive regard will be felt by the client.

In order to become a skilled and effective listener a coach needs to first encourage the client to relax. New experiences bring with them certain anxieties. The best way to encourage relaxation is with your own demonstration. I would advise the use of a question early in the process that inquires about formality.

"Would it be ok if we keep our sessions as informal as possible?" "I find that the less formal we are, the more productive the sessions seem to be, is it ok for us to just kick back and talk a bit?"

How you start will go a long way toward an enjoyable coaching process and successful conclusion.

Learn to listen. That causes people to feel comfortable and look forward to talking with you. In the opening session explore a wide array of areas until obvious coaching focal points of interests present themselves. While this skill is of utmost importance, teaching active listening is not the goal of this book. Sources to learn Active Listening are innumerable and available, through books, You Tube, and more. Take full advantage, this is very important. I will, however, list some helpful concepts for you that will help enhance your listening skills.

When coaching over the phone:

As in person, keep a number of tested open-ended questions prepared to use throughout early sessions.

Use body language, though it is not seen it keeps you in the present and that presence can be felt by the client.

Be as genuine as possible.

Respond appropriately to the client's emotionally charged moments.

During periods of silence, use the question, "Are you just thinking about it now?" Although this is a closed-end question; it may help if you are not sure whether a time of silence is actually productive.

When coaching face to face

Always have a number of tested open-ended questions prepared to use throughout early sessions.

Make eye contact frequently.

Nod in understanding, and agreement.

Refrain from folding arms.

Repeat the last sentence or last few words the client spoke during non-productive silence.

Lean forward periodically to express interest.

If you find yourself listening to issues or problems that approach a clinical pathology, it usually means the person is consulting a coach when they should be consulting a therapist. Coaches and therapists listen for very different issues.

Therapists are seeking to diagnose a DSM-V disorder, create a plan and begin treatment over several sessions. A Life Coach is listening for career, business, physical, health, and life-related goals. The coach is looking for dreams, wishful desires and what the client views as a worthwhile life pursuit.

The Miracle Question or *inquiring what it would look like if a miracle took place last night and today you are living your dream,* is a great tool to uncover life dreams. George Bernard Shaw made a great observation that both Bobby Kennedy and I have frequently converted into powerful coaching questions. He said, *"Some men see things as they are and ask why, but I dream dreams that never were and ask why not".*[iv]

Here are two questions that help clients make the decision to chase their dreams:

Can you name others who have succeeded in a similar venture? Followed by

Why not you?

This could be a risky question; but in most cases this question is more likely to solicit a positive belief rather than a list of negative excuses. While *"why"* questions are usually not the best Solution Focused Coaching questions, sometimes *"why not me"* questions have a Rational Emotive Therapy (RET) and cognitive type effect helping client's realize their capability of achieving life goals. Belief and self-confidence form the foundation for success and the springboard for victory over perceived difficulty.

Chapter summary

The importance of listening in the coaching relationship cannot be exaggerated. The foundation of coaching is listening and asking powerful questions. Carl Rogers' discovery is correct and very effective in the field of coaching. He believed that human beings are most capable of finding their own solutions to issues and formulating strategies to solve their own problems; and as a direct consequence, achieving their full potential, fulfilling deep desires; and reaching their greatest dreams.

Just as with a great athlete, good coaching brings out skills beyond what may have been exposed had coaching not taken place. A good coach has learned to listen for what those desires, potentialities, dreams, and development considerations are; and helps the client form these ephemeral items into goals and pursuits by asking the right questions. Because as a coach you listen 80% of the time, it is imperative that the best possible listening skills be developed.

Becoming an active listener involves developing skills that help the client become comfortable with you as the coach. Rogers' relationship building skills of unconditional positive regard and genuineness work much better when sincerely felt than merely imitated. Therefore a sincere appreciation for mankind is a character trait that will travel far in the coaching profession. Still you can and should develop listening skills through every available means including training and books; but mostly by applying frequent perfect practice in coaching and non-coaching conversations.

Power Questions related to Effective Listening

In the third person, tell me who is_____________? (Client's name)

Can you talk about some of the most important people in your life?

What are some of the most important things that have happened to you in your life so far?

Tell me some things you dream about and would love to do before you finish up on earth?

Chapter 3
Selecting from the
'Cream Rising to the Top'

"My father gave me the greatest gift anyone could give another person; he believed in me."

-Jim Valvano

Jim Valvano is the legendary coach of the 1983 North Carolina State National Championship Basketball Team. He created a team whose heart led them to a victory over a Hakeem Olajuwon led, University of Houston team that statistically, they did not come close to matching. Coach Valvano is most remembered for a speech that kicked off one of the greatest fundraising movements to combat cancer in our nation. Near death himself, he spoke to the 1993 ESPN sports awards gathering and said these words.

"Cancer can take away all of my physical abilities. It cannot touch my mind, it cannot touch my heart, and it cannot touch my soul."[v]

Chapter Focus

In this chapter the objective is for the coach to learn how to assist the client in choosing what are to be the **Coaching Focal Points** on which to begin to work. The coach at this point is using probing questions to facilitate the client's positive self-awareness and perspective.

A question like, "When is life frustrating for you?" reveals the client's general outlook on life. It may tell the coach that the client is a *"glass half empty"* or a *"glass half full"* thinking type person. This same question may help the coach know if the client sees things primarily from a wide-angle perspective or from a narrow perspective.

These discoveries are useful when helping the client to enhance self-awareness – the undergirding of the self-confidence needed for success. Still the primary focus sought by the coach at this stage is to come to agreement with the client regarding what the first and subsequent Coaching Focal Points should be. This chapter demonstrates a simple approach to complete that process.

Power Question: *Can you describe for me your perfect life?*

As you would guess, these words have personally inspired me to press toward reaching my greatest dreams in every area of my life. It is this quote by Coach Valvano that inspires this particular chapter concerning the cream rising to the top. I cannot think of any better gift a life coach can give to a client than to believe in them. Each session should resonate with that atmosphere and always be accomplished.

Of course our goal is for clients to believe in themselves; we want to see them grow in the confidence necessary for good people to become great. There will be ample opportunity for that to be developed to its fullest. However, without being giddy or guilty of pouring it on a bit thick; when coaches are impressed with the client's abilities and accomplishments, making it known contributes to the development of larger dreams during organized "chit-chat" and at other times.

I've been told that infants come into the world with only two fears; they are afraid of loud noises and of falling. Other fears are imposed upon them by others until they finally accept them. I wonder what that says to parent's concerning coaching kids at an early age to believe in themselves.

Think of the difference believing in one's innate abilities before being inundated with crippling fear could make in building determined children.

Over 60 years ago, I had the great fortune of hearing something only one time that stuck with me all of my life and has influenced all I do. I was under 11 years old and had just cornered my younger brother, grabbed some old manual hand hair clippers, and trimmed his hair. It actually looked ok.

Later I was in a room and overheard my mother speaking to a neighbor in another room. Not knowing I could hear her, I heard her refer to me by my nickname, CW. She was speaking about the haircut and said, "…*that CW can do anything he puts his mind to.*" From that day forward and still to this day, I believe that! In some cases the beginning of belief in oneself begins or is at least enhanced, through the voiced belief others have in you.

I've seen hard core coaching styles that assume that clients due to their current levels of success do not need this form of verbal edification. That's when my therapist training steps up and says how wrong that is. While it is true that one of the hallmarks of coaching is that we work with mentally "well" persons who do not have a mental health diagnosis; how many people do you know that do not at some time in life deserve a diagnosis, or at least show tendencies toward a mental disorder. I can assure you that if you coach long enough you will work with a client who may not have been diagnosed with major depressive disorder, but for this session they are pretty depressed.

A few probing Rational Emotive Therapy type questions may just be what the doctor ordered. These type questions force clients to consider what is actually happening; verses how they are interpreting what is happening. This approach may just rescue your session.

When you impose questions inviting the client's consideration and vocalization of recent successes, it will move the session into a more productive mode as well.

As organized chit chat progresses, certain subjects, themes, and even dreams will begin to surface.

The right questions will reveal levels of feelings and the intensity related to certain subjects. This will help with the choice of coaching focal points. Choosing what is to be coached, like most everything else involved with coaching, is at the discretion of the client—remember he or she is the expert. However the intuitive coach should influence what is to be coached through probing questions. The coach from an outside perspective is going to observe greater client potential in a variety of areas other than the client will see initially.

Your client has come to you with some very specific areas and items in mind. It would be less than professional to ignore any of these and try to impose what you believe to be a better pursuit for the client, unless the client insists upon changing his or her mind.

I believe a client comes to a session holding three levels of coaching opportunities. The first is what *they* want. The client is at a certain level in their life, career, and relationships; and now wants more. They are at least willing to hear more about life coaching to discover if this may provide an avenue to attain certain life desires.

Some of these "wants" are specific, and the wise coach will take them seriously. It could be a better job, career change, or business venture. What the client presents in the initial session of coaching are the first Coaching Focal Points to be noted and considered. The client's presented coaching desires are the first coaching focal points to be considered.

There are tools and instruments that may be used prior to or during sessions to help uncover some of the needed coaching focal points. The "Wheel of Life" is one of the widely used tools for this purpose; created by Paul J. Meyer, founder of Success Motivation® Institute, Inc. The instrument targets areas of the client's life and indicates which ones are out of balance.

Often the client's desired Coaching Focal Points require certain steps to accomplish; a good coach will often discover other coaching areas of opportunity which are germane to the success of the client's voiced coaching wants. This is the second level of coaching opportunities; I call **"coaching needs."**

Usually it is not difficult to offer powerful questions

to the client causing him/her to realize that there are other areas that need to be considered. These areas may only require short term coaching but must be dealt with in order to facilitate and further enhance the likelihood of success with primary coaching focal points. Coaching needs can take the form of objectives or strategic steps. Whether they are baby steps or large steps determines how much direct coaching is needed to effect these changes.

As an example, should someone who is habitually late want to be coached relative to a job promotion; a powerful question may lead to steps toward changing the promptness problem and making the promotion goal more realistic.

The third coaching consideration is the "**should consider issue**." This is what floats my boat but must be approached carefully. I am a life coach because my joy in life is watching people reach their greatest dreams.

I started a church nearly 30 years ago for the purpose of helping people reach their God given dreams. That is why the name of the church is New Vision. Any movie that involves someone overcoming great odds to obtain something they have worked hard and long to achieve brings on my flood gates. Therefore "Rudy" is among my favorite movies, and Kyle Maynard's "No Excuses" among my favorite books.

One of my favorite quotes is,

" circumstances don't make or break a person; they merely

Oliver Wendell Holms said, *"The great American tragedy is that most men and women go to their grave with their music still in them."* I once heard the powerfully motivating Myles Monroe speaking on this subject and attesting to the fact that the graveyard is the richest place on earth. It is full to the brim with songs never sung, businesses never started, books and poems never written, inventions never created, and dreams never pursued.

When coaching, if you listen well, you will notice a lot of cream coming to the top. That is to say the coach may see potential the client may not realize exists or has been dormant so long that the client has forgotten these dreams, desires and wishes that ever existed. The more focused and consistent the listening is on the part of the coach, the more this area will reveal a wealth of the client's core desires.

Remember, the client is the expert; you are the coach. For example, in athletic coaching, I don't believe a coach would try to convince Tiger Woods that he should give up golf and take up basketball. This Coaching Focal Point is somewhat fragile and should be carefully approached. I am not talking about suggesting career changes although in life coaching such questioning is more appropriate than in professional sports.

Sometime during organized chit chat, abilities, talents, even dreams once cast aside can again come to the surface. The right questions could rekindle a fire that could not only change focus, but may change an attitude, a life, and an income problem. The founder of the 700 Club Pat Roberson tells a story of an impoverished woman coming to him for help. After some conversation he asked her two very powerful questions. First, he asked *"Is there any skill that you have?"* She responded that she knows how to make Christmas Ornaments from eggshells. He looked at one and was very impressed. His next question was, *"Could you sell these?"*

These simple yet powerful questions surfaced a skill that enabled this woman to climb out of poverty and move upward into realizing financial security through her abilities and thus fulfilling her potential. The rest of the story is this lady did tremendously well financially and came out of poverty after responding to two powerful probing questions excavating her abilities, her dream, and her potential.

It is certainly up to the coach to decide if it is irresponsible to lead a client past the initial Coaching Focal Points initially presented by the client and delve further.

No one should be critical of a coach who helps the client realize and act upon these initial areas in the first session; and only does that. Some coaching schools may insist upon never doing that.

I would not be a coach if I were totally limited to coaching only what the client initially brought to the first session. I do believe a coach should tread lightly and not overstep the bounds of who is the expert; however a good coach with a genuine caring spirit of positive regard can probe to help excavate and unfreeze even greater potential for the client's future without crossing the line of who is the expert.

Each human being is endowed with the seeds of greatness in some area. Difficult life circumstances and negative people have assisted them to bury those seeds ever so deeply. Even if that greatness tries to sprout, it goes unnurtured. Unencouraged. Never developed. A good life coach will go to great lengths to empower the client to germinate those seeds.

Empowering involves *never blaming* and never making the client feel their current self-valuation is their fault. The skillful coach will learn how to ask questions that cause the client to reconsider certain conclusions without experiencing the negative effects of feeling foolish or blamed.

If you ever want to be recognized as an effective life coach, learn to empower your clients. If I were to sum up the entire coaching field with one word, I would choose *"empowerment."* The success of a life coach rests upon applying these techniques with electricity. Regardless of how potentially powerful electricity is, it is useless until someone pulls a switch and releases its power.

Releasing the power within another human being through conversation is a recent and acknowledged discovery shown to have enormous value to free the human spirit and allow it to soar. In the past few decades human beings have discovered the enormous value of those who are able to through conversation, release the power housed within other humans.

The great racehorse Secretariat won the 1973 Triple Crown, winning the Belmont stakes by 31 links in a time of 2 minutes and 24 seconds; a record that still stands today. The movie, *Secretariat,* is about two winning underdogs. Secretariat and its owner Penny Chenery. Trainer Lucien Laurin plan was to hold Secretariat back so the horse would not tire before the home stretch. *Secretariat* sprinted to the lead without prompting. Sensing a loss of control, Laurin screamed to Jockey Ron Turcotte to:

"Just let him run, let him run"

There are things your clients are born to do, but fear, negativity, and past failures have caused them to proceed with so much caution that it prevents success. Clients need someone to empower them and just let them run. Let them Run!

Here is a simple way a coach can best serve a client through empowerment. A low-level empowerment tool is the simple compliment related to an observation. It's simple. Just say, "There is something about you I like." Even though it is low level, it is effective. This will work.

The   next   level   of   empowerment   is   the acknowledgement. Point out something the client did and become genuinely enthused about it. I'm sure unemotional, rigid mono-toned coaching works for some people, but not for most.

The third and highest level of empowerment is the endorsement. Whenever you have an opportunity, express to your client your willingness to endorse them on some level or in some way that says you've got my vote. Remember the client is the expert; they are really good, just wanting to get better. You, as coach are helping them to get better; it only makes sense that you believe in them. When clients know you believe in them, they become more empowered to achieve the goals agreed upon in the coaching sessions. After all, how do you feel when you are acknowledged, complimented, and endorsed?

Reframing

Clients sometimes tend to create awful scenarios or catastrophes and introduce problems and negativity into the coaching session. This negative introduction or awfulizing is the act of believing that a situation is much worse than it actually is. Such a small percentage of the bad things we think will actually happen the way we expect them to. Even that low percentage is influenced by the fact that we believe and expect the worst, far too often. It doesn't take a psychologist to spot a person who has an invisible "kick me" sign on their forehead.

People like that expect the worst to happen in every

situation.

It is that "kick me" attitude that aligns the negative forces of the universe leading to the self-fulfillment of the client's negative prophecy of doom. Awfulizing on some level is done by all of us; however there are some who awfulize nearly every situation, bringing continuous disaster into their lives.

There is a proverb that says, *"Guard your heart with all diligence for out of it flows the issues of life."*[vi] To awfulize is to think thoughts of increased negativity related to an occurrence or circumstance. Awfulizing leads to irrational thinking that leads to negative speech and is no friend of success.

Virginia Satir, the great 20th century therapist, and developer of the Conjoint Family therapeutic approach once said, *"All meaning is self-create*d." People often create the worst possible scenarios in their minds, and subconsciously instruct their bodies to go make them happen. This process has been called "catastrophic predicting." It feels safer because it allows one to gradually feel the letdown and disappointment of failure or of a negative experience before it occurs. Let me repeat that. It feels safer because it allows one to gradually feel the letdown and disappointment of failure or of a negative experience before it occurs. Terms like, don't get your hopes up, don't set yourself up to be hurt, or prepare for the worst, are considered catastrophizing a person's best wisdom. People are often cowards and fearful of emotional pain.

That is why Emotional Intelligence quotient levels are important in predicting and insuring client success. Should coaches try to cushion hurt with too many questions inviting catastrophic predicting this may greatly hinder client success. What this does is create negative results through the lack of belief and self-confidence. While it may feel somewhat safe to expect the worst, catastrophic prediction assists the client in the destruction of his or her own bright future.

When addressing awfulizing and catastrophic predicting, the solution-focused coach knows how to reframe such client conversation. This is done through powerful reframing questions moving the client to consider alternate perspectives to this negative, problem-oriented thinking. Williams and Menendez states that,

> *"When you reframe as a coach, you find an authentic way to put a positive spin on an issue."*
>
> -Williams and Menendez (2007).

Reframing involves the creation of an entirely new language for the client's use. When the client hears the alternate approach coming from his or her own voice it has the effect of changing outlook and even belief. Whatever emotion is fed is the emotion that grows and dominates.

The coach should not allow the client to soak up the negative influences of defeated speech but should instead introduce other powerful positive options for consideration. Questions like, can you describe a more positive way you could look at this, if you chose to find some good in this, what would it be; or if this is a test what will be the benefits once you pass it?

The coach's attitude of expectant success can offer the client the support, endorsement and empowerment needed to compel the client to consider themselves as very capable of handling and gaining from the challenges of the current circumstances rather than being stymied or halted by them.

Coach Um Up, Coach!

A few months ago I had an inspiring conversation with the Auburn University Basketball Coach, and former ESPN analyst, Bruce Pearl. Coach Pearl is certainly one of the most motivated people I've ever come across. It really does not matter what Coach Pearl is involved with, expect an elevated level of intensity and enthusiasm to arrive when he shows up.

As I shared with him my commitment to foster and adopt children his enthusiasm was nearly as strong as mine for the opportunity to affect the lives of hurting kids more likely to go to prison than to finish college.

I have no idea where I first heard the phrase *"Coach um up, Coach,"* but I like it. The concept assumes that a good athletic or life coach, who is skilled, can help another human being perform tasks, achieve goals, and live dreams they otherwise may have never achieved.

In the beginning of this book I wrote these words. *"It seems silly to think Tiger Woods, Michael Jordan, and Peyton Manning for all of their careers continued to insist upon more and more coaching, unless you clearly understand that "only coaching can excavate deeply concealed greatness- in sports and in life."* What is exciting about solution focused coaching is its awesome success in facilitating human achievement and significant levels of greatness.

An amazing reality of creation is the process of metamorphosis. Psychologists have used the term cocooning to describe human similarities to certain activities of the butterfly. When people withdraw mentally, slow down and reflect, a renewal process is initiated; and the formulation of significant transformational change emerges.

Once a butterfly lays an egg, the tiny caterpillar begins to eat its way through, and forms its own cocoon from the silk which it produces. Soon the caterpillar has eaten enough to sustain itself while making metamorphic changes inside the cocoon, leading to chrysalis or the shaping of an entirely new and different form.

Everything that composes a beautiful butterfly is in place, yet it remains wrapped in confinement for 5 days to 8 months. Finally it goes through the molting or de-clothing stage and out comes one of God's most beautiful creations, a vibrant, colorful, confident, and gentle, butterfly.[vii]

It is during this symbolic molting and de-clothing human stage that the client usually comes to coaching and the life coach earns his/her worth. Clients come to coaching with everything needed to succeed in their chosen field of endeavor, buried deep inside them, awaiting excavation and the journey to the surface.

Coach um up, Coach! Use motivational, empowering, and challenging questions to draw out of the client the zeal, enthusiasm, and desire to achieve the greatness that is in us all. This is what Martin Luther King Jr. referred to as "*The Drum Major Instinct;*" the innate desire to move out front. This desire or "want to" most likely still exists to some degree and at some level; even though problems, issues, troubles, and rejection suggest otherwise. Coach um up Coach!

Chapter 4
Visualization: Helping clients to see themselves living it.

"I never hit a shot, not even in practice, without having a very sharp in-focus picture of it in my head".

-Jack Nicklaus

Jack Nicklaus is one of the greatest golfers to ever play. He won 18 Major Golf tournaments during his career that spanned more than four decades as a professional, including 6 Masters Competitions.

Chapter Focus

In this chapter you will learn of the tremendous value of visualization related to success. You will discover techniques and powerful questions designed to help your clients to use visualization to maintain a positive outlook and the mental image necessary to reach their goals and dreams.

Power Question: If while you were sleeping tonight a miracle happened and you woke up living your dream tomorrow what things would be changed.

Willie Mays made one of the greatest catches in the history of baseball during the 1954 World Series. The New York Giants were playing the Cleveland Indians at the Polo Grounds in New York. There are some who believe Mays was the greatest to ever play the game.

Willie had this philosophy when he played; he did not like giving up what we have come to call Texas League Singles. Those are fly balls that drop about midway between the infield and the outfield's warning track. Willie felt that if he played a shallow centerfield, he could stop those Texas Leaguers from dropping.

He also believed that he was fast enough to run toward the fence and shag anything that was hit over his head. Well with the score tied in the eighth inning, Vic Wertz hit a ball well over Willie's head destined to land against the fence and give the Indians a late inning lead. Larry Doby, certain the ball would not be caught, did not tag but instead darted for third intending to head for home to score the go ahead run.

When Mays caught the ball, Doby had to rush back, tag second and could only make it as far as third base.[viii] Recalling the moment, Mays often referred to it as not being that difficult, like a lot of other great feats at the crack of the bat, he saw himself doing it; that's Visualization.

The Coach who can help clients to see themselves actually doing the thing they are being coached to do is miles ahead of the game.

The Miracle Question and "Poof" are great tools to accomplish this. The Miracle Question visualizes the morning after a miracle takes place relative to the client's goals.

"Poof "works similarly. Early in the coach/client relationship, establish rather playfully, the agreement that every time you as coach says 'Poof', everything stops, a magic feat has occurred and the client must now see and feel themselves living their dream.

The Coach request that it be described in the first person, singular, present tense—

"I am speaking to an audience of 5000 and owning them".

This is likely to be met each time with humor, but will still be effective, especially if the coach insists on the client's elaboration. Remember the proverb, *"laughter does good like medicine."*[ix]

Other powerful questions to consider are, "What things will be different when you reach your goal? What are some of the good things that will occur once you achieve this? If you did a quick brainstorm what would be on a list of positive changes once you reach this dream, goal, etc.? Once you've done this, how will it affect your level of self-fulfillment?

The power of visualization creates the positive mental attitude needed to succeed. Emmitt Smith the great Dallas Cowboy Running Back speaks about how he became great with these two quotes on visualization:

"Dreaming means 'rehearsing' what you see, playing it over and over in your mind until it becomes as real to you as your life right now." "I used to imagine what it would be like to do what Jim Brown was doing. I used to imagine what it would be like to be like a Tony Dorsett. I used to imagine what it would be like to be like Walter Payton. I was imagining Emmitt Smith doing exactly what they were doing."[x]

Children come into the world with everything needed to be tremendous successes in life. By the time they get through their adolescent years, parents and society have molded many of them into fearful, uncertain, low self-esteemed beings, who are very willing to settle for much less than their God given potential.

Many adults live nearly all of their lives stuck in adolescence. You know the place! It's where kids and adults desire and demand the things which certain maturity and age levels qualifies them for; yet are unwilling to accept the responsibilities related to acquiring and maintaining those things. In adulthood, people often adopt small goals with low expectations and are unwilling to invest the time, effort, and energy necessary to reach big dreams; or perhaps they just don't believe they can.

In the early 1990's, I was approached by a football player who was great but had never won a championship on any level. He asked me to help him with a goal he had, related to working with youth at risk. After great success a few months later he asked me to continue to work with him as we had already started a friendship.

Reggie White is gone now but I have great memories of the tremendous life he shared with all of us. I recall a time in my home when Reggie was urging his daughter Jecolia to kiss my son Ethan. At the time, they were both about 4 and 5 years old. Neither of them was interested, but we all had a great laugh. Laughter was hugely important to Reggie and me and we did our share of it.

Anyone who knew Reggie knew him as a great dreamer. He seemed to have this visualization thing down better than most. The truth is Reggie thought he could do anything and would try it if someone did not stop him. He was a dreamer.

When Reggie was playing in Philadelphia, knowing I am a lifetime Dallas Cowboy's fan, he invited me up to a Monday night Game; the Eagles were playing the Cowboys. My wife and I left Reggie's home in New Jersey and headed to Veterans Memorial Stadium where I had my first encounter with tens of thousands hostile Cowboy haters. Of course, the Eagles killed the Cowboys that night and I never lived it down.

Fast forward several months and Reggie and I are in his home in Tennessee late one evening talking about where he will play the following year. This was the end of all of the courting teams had been doing, trying to get him to sign with them after his free agent year. Just before I left for home, he spoke about how Art Modell of the Cleveland Browns had spared no expense in receiving him for a visit. I was totally convinced that Reggie would be signing with the Browns the next day

He actually told me that was what he was going to do and asked what I thought. Now I know that was just a friend-to-friend question, he did not care what I wanted. If it were up to me, he would have been a Cowboy for life. But I responded saying, *"Reggie, what do you ultimately want to accomplish?"*

The next day I was shocked to learn that he had signed with the Green Bay Packers. I asked him a powerful question; did it have anything to do with his decision, I will never know and frankly, I lean toward, probably not. But unless he was snowing some of his closest friends at that time, sometime during the night he made a decision that lead him to two Super Bowl Championships. After years of dreaming and believing from high school, through college into the NFL he finally reached his dream of being a champion in Green Bay, Wisconsin.

Coach your clients to dream big if they are going to dream at all.

One of my greatest hero's Denis Waitley said,

"Close your eyes and visualize the person you really want to be, who fits your own concepts of self-respect. If you can see the person clearly in the mirror of your mind, you surely will become that person."

Visualization is like a trip to the Disney World. There is so much to choose from, and all of it exciting, refreshing, exhilarating and blissful. For some brief period after visiting Disney World, one maintains a portion of those exciting emotions. Most of us won't visit Disney World but once, twice or a few times in life.

However, you can vicariously visit your goals and dreams as often as you'd like in your mind. Everything that ever existed was created in the mind before it appeared in the natural setting. As a life coach one of the greatest services you can give to your client is to help them use solitude to see themselves achieving their desires, goals, and dreams.

The work of Daniel Goleman and others has helped us to understand that Emotional Intelligence Quotient (EQ) is very possibly as important as intelligence Quotient (IQ) related to achievement and dream chasing. People with high EQs run a much better chance of not quitting prematurely and thus, achieving their dreams.[xi]

My experience has been that there is a great emotional benefit today dreaming about positive things. Meditating and daydreaming about what it's like to actually be doing the thing you want to do the most, brings with it a vicariously refreshing emotional feeling every time.

Dr. David McClelland in his work on achievement motivation maintains that people do well, when they emotionally feel good. Whether we choose to call it daydreaming, creative visualization or pensiveness; we have the ability to take ourselves into deep thought on a subject of our own choosing. Of course hypnotherapists may take this further.

I am insisting that as a life coach, the more time your client spends in deep thinking about a time when the goal is achieved, the better the chances of attaining it. There is a wonderful Proverb that says, "As a man thinketh in his heart, so is the man."

Part of your responsibility as a life coach is to help client's to stretch. Coach them to change their perception of self and of opportunities. The unchallenged mind must filter opportunities through its perceived limits. Challenge your clients to break though the limits of their conditioned mind. Consider this poem.

I bargained with life for a penny. And life would pay no more
However I begged at evening when I counted my scanty store.
For life is a just employer. He gives you what you ask.
But once you have set the wages, why you must bear the task.

I worked for a menial's hire, only to learn dismayed,
That any wage I had asked of life, Life would have willingly paid.

-(Unknown)

Legend has it that when Albert Einstein was asked for his phone number, he went to a phone book and found it & repeated it to the inquirer. Mr. Einstein thought it pointless to take up space in his mind with information he could easily find elsewhere.

To us, for the man who unlocked the hidden laws of General Relativity, ($E=mc^2$) this may seem a little stupid. It really seems ridiculous when one considers that researchers believe Einstein, like all of us, used only a fraction of his brain's creative capacity during his life of world changing accomplishments.

Neither you nor your client should allow your life to be a meaningless pilgrimage seeking only a return to dust. Choose carefully what you allow to dominate your mind. I urge you to value your usefulness as a life coach and don't go to your grave with your music still in you, having bargained with life for only a penny.

Oliver Wendell Holmes Jr. said, *"Man's mind once stretched to a new idea never regains its original dimensions."*

How have you stretched your mind lately? I'm just asking.

Chapter 5
Establishing Winning Strategies,

"Persistence can change failure into extraordinary achievement."

– Marv Levy

Marv Levy coached the Buffalo Bills of the National Football League to achieve 123 wins and four straight Super Bowl appearances. During his career he won 6 division titles and 4 AFC championships. He is a powerful motivational speaker and is greatly respected by his coaches and peers. Thurman Thomas, former All-Pro Buffalo Bills Running Back said of him,

"Coach Levy is one of the most inspirational people that I have ever known."[xii]

Chapter Focus

The goal of this chapter is to teach the coach to draw out of the client strategies for reaching the identified goals of coaching. The client is *always* the expert not the coach. The client within him or herself has all he or she needs to successfully reach their greatest dreams. Coaches are responsible for facilitating an atmosphere that draws the goals, strategies, and steps to the surface through powerful questions.

There are two effective solution focused tools which expedite this process. One is **Scaling Questions**. After learning how to use scaling questions the coach is well equipped to assist the client as he or she chooses the goals to be pursued. Scaling questions facilitates the development of thoughts about methods of achieving client goals. They also act as a barometer measuring a client's perceived progress toward the goals session by session.

The second tool is the technique involving the use of empowerment through acknowledgment of what the client already does well or what he or she is doing right that can help with success. I call this accentuating the positive.

After hearing about what a client is doing well right now, ask the power question; how could you make certain that you do more of that?

Use of Scaling Questions

A great tool for establishing strategy is Scaling Questions. In order to solicit client goals and evoke action provoking thoughts, use scaling questions. Scaling questions are used to determine where the client feels he/she lands on a scale from one to ten related to their progress towards a specific coaching focal point or a potential focal point.

I usually give clients a pen and draw a continuum. I asked them to circle the number coinciding with their perceived level of progress reached. Then I circle a number usually 2 or sometimes 3 numbers higher and ask, *"What would it take to get you there?"* Of course this is the beginning of the coach drawing out of the client steps, strategies, weaknesses, and strengths.

A skillful use of Scaling Questions will yield enormous amounts of information related to secondary coaching focal points. Secondary coaching focal points involve strategies to replace goal impeding habits, with habits which enhance the achievement of the larger coaching goals.

I use scaling questions both written and verbal to establish goals and to empower clients to reach goals. They work well as a weekly measurement of a client's progress and as motivational tools. I would point out that the obvious concern with scaling questions is when the client has to reveal that he or she has stagnated or regressed.

Remember this is Solution focused, not failure or regression focused coaching. What went wrong is never a question to be asked. Even a negative look on the face of the coach is not a solution focused approach.

A good habit in coaching is to never dwell on the opposite of what you want to see from your client. There are times especially early in the coaching relationship when problems are discussed to some length. Even then, positivity and hope should dominate the atmosphere. When the client has to report stagnation or regression relative to a goal, the coach does nothing to in any way punish or show disappointment. It is at this point that the coach, with much belief and expectation, draws from the client another numerical goal for the next week.

This could be followed with questions like,

"Is there anything you think you should do differently this week?" "Are all the steps you established still the best ones, if not what new steps shall we explore?"

Even this must be done carefully to not give off a negative response or doubtful temperament. It would be better to completely ignore the regression and simply scale for the next week, if negativity cannot be avoided.

Accentuating the Positive

A huge component of solution focused coaching is to motivate the client to do more of what they have already done that has contributed to goal attainment in the past.

Not long ago as I was watching an old movie on television called *Here Comes the Waves*. Soon the old crooner Bing Crosby was singing a tune written in 1944 by Harold Arlen and Johnny Mercer called **Accentuate the Positive**. I have kind of taken that as my mantra. When things are not going as I'd like them to, I often sing the words of that song to its very catchy and uplifting melody. As a solution focused coach you have got to master the ability of coaching clients into spending as much time focusing on *what is working*, being encouraged, and then continuing to more of that action(s).

One of the best ways of making this happen is to do what the great North Carolina Tar heels coach did. Dean Smith coached some of the greatest players to ever play the game of basketball, including James Worthy, Eric Montross, Kenney Smith, and the best of all times, Michael Jordan. In answering questions concerning his success and how it came about, Coach Smith gave a very simple response; he said, *"I praise behavior I want to see repeated!"* Wow, what a great solution focused concept. It works! Praise what you want to see repeated.

As a coach when you are able to get your clients to reveal what is working, the next step is to get them to not only keep doing it, but, if possible, to increase it. Praise, compliments, and endorsements serve as great motivational tools empowering the client to do more of the same.

The solution focused approach does not dwell on the problem; it spends the greater portion of the coaching process on *discovering and chasing solutions*. Because clients are usually well functioning and have come to you seeking ways to progress even further, see that as an indicator, signaling that they have done a number of things right. It is not difficult to find out what those things are; simply ask.

The client's response to that question causes an emotional uplift through positive self-awareness and through building self-esteem, emanating from now seeing oneself in a positive light. When clients feel good, they do good. The strategies, ideas and steps that erupt from a motivated, enthusiastic, and positively expectant client are the foundation and substance of success.

Ask questions like,

"What are you doing that you feel good about right now?"
"What *things have been working for you in the past?"*
"What did that accomplishment look and feel like?"
"When have you not had this concern, what was that like?"

Remembering Who Is in Charge Here

Solution Focused Coaching works because the client is the expert. I continue to make this point because a well-meaning coach could take any of the techniques and overzealously begin to do more teaching, lecturing, and mentoring than is involved in Solution Focused Coaching. Our strong belief is that through coaching people are capable of accomplishing much more in life than could be accomplished by lecturing in order to change a client's self-defeating and belittling beliefs and attitudes. That usually shows up through the session moving more toward a 50/50 speaking ration than an 80/20 percent ratio with the client speaking most of the time, as it should be. [Establishing an 80/20 (Client/Coach) speaking ration rather than a 50/50 speaking ratio will lay the groundwork for keeping the client in charge of their progress and having the joy of ownership as goals are realized.]

The coach should use powerful questions to facilitate the client's description of what he or she wants; and, in most cases the coach should be content with that. Clients may at a later time, after reaching the agreed goal, seek something more challenging; it is all up to the expert; the client.

Chapter Summary:

For a solution focused plan to become a winning strategy it has to come from within the client. Coaches have to trust that the client knows best what they want to become and what it takes to get there. Coaches are always bringing out the best of what is inside the client. Scaling Questions and Accentuating the Positive are two techniques that will produce sound strategies and motivate clients to achieve their goals and dreams.

As with any coaching skill, the more experience coaches have with the techniques the more competent they are at applying them. These are two techniques that should be used not only in each session, but several times during each session.

Chapter 6
Communication: It's your best Tool

"*Effective teamwork begins and ends with communication.*"

-Mike Krzyzewski

Mike Krzyzewski will not only go down in history as one of the greatest college coaches; having 12 National Coach of the Year titles, but he will also be known as one of America's great caring and compassionate human beings.

Chapter Focus

Effective communication involves three very distinct skills. The first is *active listening* which was covered in Chapter 1. Active listening creates an atmosphere where the client is comfortable enough to reveal his/her innermost thoughts to the coach.

The second skill involved with communication is *accurate interpretation*. Communication is not solely what is being said, it is what is heard and understood. The English language is complicated for a number of reasons; one is the numbers of homonyms.

Another reason is punctuation, which can only be seen in written words and must be assumed in spoken language. A simple example would be," Close the door!" Or "Close the door." Or "Close the Door?" Depending upon the punctuation the written three-word phrase could denote anger as in "Close the door!" It may imply a soft kindness even though there is no "please" in front as in "Close the door." It could also be used as a question with an understood (did you) "Close the door?"

In verbal communication for the most part, Americans have adjusted well to this, but still have many communication problems. One of the difficulties in communicating for persons using English or any other dialect as a second language is the placing of verbal punctuations in places where most people speaking the native tongue, don't place them; especially accent marks. This can even cause communication difficulties from region to region and culture to culture as does ever changing ethnic, cultural, and social network jargon.

Power Question: Am I correct? What I hear you saying is…?

The best communication includes the ability to evaluate what the client brings to the session and determine its probative value. Because an early session may take a number of directions in order to discover the most important coaching focal points, the coach must be skilled in placing a chronological value on the information based upon the client's input.

The use of clear, defining language expressing and reframing thoughts, goals, objectives, and concerns is of great worth. Any coach who can think quickly, relying on experience and knowledge to communicate, is well on the way to becoming an effective life coach.

A life coach should spend considerable time loading into his or her mental tool chest a number of metaphors, analogies, and very short, powerful stories covering a number of situations. In coaching, the ability to paint mental pictures has a much better chance of communicating to clients who are visual, auditory, or kinesthetic type learners. Much of life coaching is done by phone where there is no client glimpses and no physical proximity thus, creating visualizations is of enormous communicative value. Sequentially, to draw out the most logical coaching focal points, the coach interprets and gives feedback that facilitates the narrowing of broad information, into specific systems of solution focused concerns.

The third is the ability to *ask powerful questions*. A powerful question is one that evokes the client's responses related to awareness, insight, empowerment, commitment and/or action. Each of these components is paramount in the coaching relationship. This is the stuff successful coaching is made of. When coach and client team up in solid communication, it maximizes these positive components necessary for success.

Awareness

Awareness is best illustrated by the Shakespearian play *Hamlet*, Act 1 scene 3 when Polonius is watching his son Laertes boarding a boat to Paris, fleeing from one more of his father's long lectures about life. He says, *"This above all: to thine own self be true, And it must follow, as the night the day, Thou canst not then be false to any man."*[xiii] Questions asked to evoke awareness not only cause clients to consider limiting realities, they also open up realms of possibility and opportunities perhaps never before considered. Questions such as, *"Can you list for me your major strengths?"* could start a coaching session revealing more attributes and skills than the client was aware existed. These are golden nuggets that can be used to help your client reach their greatest dreams, provided the client will *"to thine own self be true."*

Insight

Insight usually involves understanding that Solution Focus Coaching is not overly concerned with the "why" of an issue; it seeks solutions, not the breaking down of problems. The simplest definition of insight relates to understanding the relationship between cause and effect in a situations or circumstance. In the broader sense, insight is a great tool to draw out from the client what does work.

There is a Proverb that states, *"Any enterprise is built upon wise planning, grows strong through common sense and profits wonderfully by staying abreast of the facts."*[xiv] Insight provides the beginnings of success over failures and the start of self-improvement. I've heard it said that *"failure is the only opportunity one has to start over, and this time be smarter,* the *'smarter'* could be described as insight. Clients come to coaching with great insight, often buried. Solution-focused coaches facilitate the excavating and surfacing of that insight without the usual accompaniment of negative connotations.

Empowerment

Empowerment is the coaching skill helping clients to see, believe and act in a manner conducive to attaining new possibilities, goals, dreams, and life modifications. In the work of John Gottman concerning negative and positive interactions in relationships, it seems that negativity has its place and is somewhat useful. However the recommended ratio of negative to positive interaction for a healthy relationship is 5 positive interactions to 1 negative. This means that 80% of clients' interactions should be positive. Since this is not too likely in the real world, the coach should spend considerable time purposefully supporting the empowerment of the client. This cheerleading aspect of coaching keeps clients in the state of mind necessary to complete the coaching process.[xv]

Commitment

Commitment questions involve inviting the client to voice his/her own levels of integrity, and character. Integrity defines who the client is when no one is looking. Character is the client's ability to carry out a commitment fully at least until the next session. In the vein of Reality and Choice Therapy, the client just agrees with the coach on what will be the pursuits, strategies, and homework between sessions. While praise and natural rewards are received by the client upon completion of goals and objectives; there should be no negative innuendoes or punishments for procrastination or a failure to complete agreed upon goals between sessions.

Counterproductive habits are difficult to replace; and dwelling on the opposite of the behavior desired does not incite change. Coaches skillfully empower clients to deploy the strategy agreed upon with zeal and determination. I usually tell my clients to make a super decision to *"do right until it feels right"* or until the *desired behavior becomes habit.*

Action

The universe only rewards action. It does not reward talk, or thoughts or good intentions. So much of coaching is talking, planning, preparation, insights and more; however, the universe only rewards action. A hungry man can surround himself with all the foods fit for a king, but unless he eats, eventually he will starve to death. Every powerful question may have a secondary purpose, such as awareness or planning strategy, however, the ultimate aim is action. When the strategy is agreed upon two other agreements should be sought immediately. One is to whom the client shall be accountable, concerning the action.

You've heard it said that people don't do what you expect, they do what you inspect. Normally this comes complete with an inspector's negative punishing approach. That is not what Solution Focused Life Coaches do. It is great to dream of self-motivated clients who will do all they sign up for; that is not what they do, which is why they hired a coach. Our goal as coaches is not to whip them into shape; it is to facilitate an atmosphere conducive to maintaining the action steps necessary to succeed.

The solution focused life coach walks softly and carries **no** stick. His/her job is to help the client to move forward with the action(s) the client has decided he wants to engage. The client wants this; therefore the coach uses powerful questions to continue to move the client back into the place that **empowers or fuels** the action. One of the methods of moving clients into the action state is through acting the part. Dennis Waitley calls it

"Practicing within, when you are without."

Some of the greatest baseball players started out using broom sticks as bats, peach seeds wrapped with tape as balls and milk cartons as gloves. I've seen kids with pencils banging on cardboard, grow up to be solid trap-set drummers.

Some powerful questions to propose to a stagnated client are, "If you reached your dream tomorrow, what would you look like?" "Can you in some way, live as though you have attained that goal?" Ask the client, "Can you step into the future? You've achieved the desired outcome. What are you doing right now? What does this picture look like?"

It is very important to the process of forwarding the action by learning to dance in the rain. A few years ago while speaking in Nassau, I was able to have a discussion with the great contemporary gospel singer Donnie McClurkin. We talked about mutual friends and a song he had written called *Stand,* which serves as a great encouragement to continue regardless of how difficult things become.

Donnie has written another song that I feel takes that notion a step further; it's called *I Choose to be Dancing*. It was Eleanor Roosevelt who said, *"No one can make you feel inferior without your permission."* The truth is no one can make you feel **any** emotion without your permission.

The life coach should use powerful, challenging questions to help the client choose to dance in the middle of a difficult time. It is often what the client is telling him or herself that slows them from positive action. If not successfully disputed, these thoughts could short circuit the success process.

The solution focused life coach through powerful questioning can influence a client to feel as they have never felt before; think as they've never thought before; and act as they've never acted before. That is what leads them to achieve what they've never achieved before.

The now retired Space Shuttles represent the most powerful mobile creations of man. The Columbia weighed more than 178,000 pounds and as were all the Space Shuttles, capable of speeds of more than 17,000 miles per hour and allowed mankind to complete feats absolutely mind boggling.[xvi] At this speed to travel from Los Angeles to New York City would take about 10 minutes. Of course by the time you hit the brakes you'd end up in London, I suppose.

However, without triggering an ignition system, these

now retired colossal space shuttles would lie dormant as nothing more than 85-ton spectacles. The right questions to the human mind are what ignitions are to the space shuttle—when triggered, they unleash enormous possibilities.

Chapter 7
The Solution Focused Coaching Process

"The only place success comes before work is in the dictionary."

- Vince Lombardi

Vincent Thomas Lombardi is arguably the greatest football coach of all time and is on the short list of history's greatest coaches, regardless of the sport. His ability to teach, motivate and inspire players helped turn the Green Bay Packers into the most dominating NFL team in the 1960s. (www.vincelombardi.com)

Chapter Focus

The goal of this chapter is to acquaint coaches with the Solution Focused Coaching process. The end result is always the successful attainment of the client's selected goals. The coach who understands the process is better equipped to facilitate the navigation and pursuit of those goals. Certain distractions and detours will naturally occur, the maintaining of forward progress is the responsibility of the client expert, but the effective coach knows to offer probing questions to insure that the client is pondering and processing how to stay on track.

Power Question: *Can you describe what you feel you have achieved so far?*

Discovery, Empowerment and Solutions

The Solution Focused Coaching process involves Discovery, Empowerment and Solutions. As mentioned earlier, active listening is the method used to discover the coaching focal points to be agreed upon. After it is clear what the client is prepared to pursue the coach can move into empowerment and solutions. Usually empowerment follows, however solutions may in some measure, come before. What's important is that the client feels a empowered related to his/her goals, dreams, problems, and pursuits. Sometimes this sensation comes prior to or during the solution search, as part of the process. I like to empower the client before solutions as it tends to create a much more positive expectant disposition and a capacity to dream larger. This usually leads to more creative, solid strategies and steps for achieving the goals and objectives surfaced during discovery.

Discovery, empowerment, and solution strategizing each require a specific type of question to ignite those segments of the coaching process.

In the discovery process, or organized chit chat, questions are asked to allow the client to explore within himself or herself an array of coaching possibilities such as things that may not have been given much thought or viewed with any degree of importance in pursuing happiness or reaching a higher goal.

At this point the problem is discussed, and it is appropriate to ask questions related to a faulty belief, or misconception that may slow the attainment of goals the client wants to reach. While solution focused coaching does not dwell on problems and negatives, some discussion of them is necessary to be able to properly address certain hindrances with a positive attitude to better protect the success of the process.

During the discovery stage the coach should ask questions such as what changes in your life would you like to make, what frustrates you right now, what would make you feel better about things, or describe how life is going these days? The skilled coach will be able to flow through a comfortable conversation asking probing questions and come away with several notes defining the client's current interests, aptitudes, abilities, concerns, issues, goals, and dreams.

I worked with a client once who was the single mother of two, living in a trailer, working in a dead-end job. It did not take very long to discover her potential even though there were scars lingering from ill treatment over years; and some rash coping skills used to combat any perceived re-surfacing of any further ill treatment. Inside was a strong, gold nugget surrounded by a self-willed, resilient spirit of determination. During one of our sessions, I asked her what it is she really wants to do with her life. After hearing her reply, I began to facilitate discussions that involved a strong consideration of the costs of her dream, related to money, time, education and more. While she was certainly not an elderly lady, should she attend college, she would not have been considered a traditional student.

To this date I have not worked with a client more willing, determined, and agreeable to the pursuit of her dream through working with the newly surfaced strategies. Within an amazingly short period of time, she went from high school graduate, to receiving first a Bachelors' degree and then a master's degree from a major university. She became the Executive Director of a seven-figure budgeted agency.

Needless to say moving from the trailer and owning a home just came with the territory, along with many other achievements. I recall that there were people who felt it their responsibility to protect her against the pangs of disappointment that come with chasing something you won't ever achieve. There are always well-meaning people trying to victimize clients into what Zig Ziglar called a "SNIOP"- **S**ensitive to the **N**egative **I**nfluences of **O**ther **P**eople.

This is when the life coach becomes the coach in every strong sense of the word and with the client creates a strategy to combat outside negative forces. Coaching uses powerful and insightful questions to bring to the surface, deeply concealed dreams, potential and life development goals; and then with more questions, holds the dreamer responsible for creating strategies to chase and seize them all.

During the times of empowerment building, coaches use powerful questions to raise the level of client belief and confidence. When these two forces are in place clients have a much greater likelihood of reaching their goals. It is for this reason that the coach must use powerful questions to draw out from within the client a positive attitude based upon truth. The empowerment questions are always designed to facilitate the client toward recalling past victories and how they came about. He or she is also encouraged to dream and think of what things would look like if a miracle took place and "you woke up living your dream."

Several years ago I was approached by a vibrant young man who told me he wanted to start a church. Well, I have to tell you honestly. A coach does not have to be an expert in the client's chosen field of endeavor remember, the client is always the expert. However, it certainly does not hurt to be an expert in the same field as the client as long as the coach avoids lecturing, session domination and too much advising.

Having started a very successful church nearly four decades ago I could not resist asking some not particularly appropriate coaching questions. I said, "Why?" I suppose my mind went back to the most difficult aspects and did not immediately think about the fire in my belly that pushed me to pursue that Vision from God.

After quickly recovering, I begin to ask some very well-informed powerful coaching questions. I was able to ask questions that perhaps a coach who was less experienced in ministry would not have been able to ask. Over a period of more than one year I coached this young man through decisions, strategies, objectives, and steps that eventually lead to the opening of his new church, which stands today as a vibrant growing church several years after its birth.

Questions used to empower clients are similar to these:

"What things will be different once you achieve this dream or goal?" "How would you explain what your life would be like once you accomplish this?" "Describe for me a time when you have succeeded and were proud?"

The entire function of what the coach does is summed up in Solution Focused questioning. Everything else leads to strategies, plans and steps suggested by the client. The client is the expert responsible for planning strategies, solving issues, and reaching goals. When a session is going well the coach is able to sit and enjoy the client go on and on about possible solutions until settling in on a strategy.

You can almost literally see the wheels of the client's mind whirling like a spinning top as one idea after another surfaces from the gold mine between his or her ears. Adrenalin begins to rush, dopamine is activated, endorphins are released, and the creative juices all begin to flow.

Chapter 8
Why Solution Focused Coaching Works

"Success comes from knowing that you did your best to become the best that you are capable of being."

- John Wooden

One of the most revered coaches in the history of sports, Wooden was beloved by his former players, among them Kareem Abdul-Jabbar and Bill Walton. Wooden was renowned for his short, simple inspirational messages to his players, including his "Pyramid of Success."[xvii] These messages often were directed at how to be a success in life as well as in basketball.

Chapter Focus

Solution Focused Coaching, like Solution Focused Therapy works because it takes what the mind naturally does in problem solving and enhances it. Venting is not only therapeutic, but also refreshing, and empowering. When we talk aloud, in response to the right questions, our mind demonstrates its tremendous creative abilities. The goal of this chapter is to describe how the coach brings out the best in the client and to demonstrate how this form of coaching facilitates the formation of new success producing habits.

Power Question: *How have you managed to fight through obstacles in the past?*

Coaching New Habits and Client Resilience

It is the combination of several major factors that causes Solution Focused Coaching to log large numbers of successes. First some of the best aspects of Solution Focused, Person Centered and Cognitive Behavioral therapies are used. The methods and successes associated with Solution Focused Therapy are easily transferable to Solution Focused Coaching. Any coach who is accustomed to asking powerful questions simply learns to not dwell on the problems and to facilitate the finding of solutions and the subsequent strategizing for solutions.

Out of this method comes a more positive atmosphere that causes the client to function with more expectation, enhancing the client's ability to change failure-producing habits into habits producing success. The value of a good habit is immeasurable; yet most habits were formed accidentally. Anything you do for 3 or 4 weeks in the same way generally becomes a habit and when threatened, usually fights long enough and strongly enough to maintain itself.

Ever tried to put first through your shirt, the arm you normally put in last? It's weird because you never do that.

There are many habits you perform not because it's the best way; it is simply your way. Some of us even have the nerve to prejudge others who do things differently. Habits, good or bad, control us and determine life's successes and failures. Whether habits involve eating, sleeping, procrastination, prayer, work habits, or commitment levels, most people fail in their efforts to create new ones.

The fact that a habit change sparks movement toward health, happiness, and success alone is not motivation enough to invoke changes. It is only possible to replace bad habits with good habits, through the maintenance of consistency, which is enhanced through coaching accountability.

Also, Solution Focused Coaching espouses methods and techniques enhancing resilience—a component essential for attaining client goals. Unfortunately people struggle in alarming rates with success hindering responses to stress and adversity; we overeat, over medicate and under achieve. I read a story once of a huge flock of seagulls living in a certain ocean shore area. Each generation thrived on the fish that they skillfully stalked, attacked and consumed. With laser-like precision each of those seagulls would dart headfirst into the ocean and rise again with a mature fish trapped inside its mouth.

Soon a hatchery sets up shop near where the seagulls hunted and begins to discard a large amount of dead unused fish from the hatchery. The seagulls begin to feast each day never having to put forth any effort to hunt anymore. As the story goes, the hatchery one day closed down and now the present generation of seagulls never learned to hunt and began to die of starvation.

Finally someone got the idea to bring other seagulls into the area who then demonstrated the hunting skills which had been lost to the other birds. After a short time the skill was as sharp as ever among the seagulls inhabiting that shore.

Humans seem to be on a never-ending mission to make everything in life easier. None of us would be quick to give up the conveniences of the twenty-first century as relates to mechanics and technology. How could we live without microwaves, computers, cars, cell phones and television? I am presently sitting at my computer typing what you are now reading. I don't know if people living in a less automated era, with few or no technological advances, were more or less resilient than this generation.

What I do know is emotional intelligence producing

resilience is necessary for our growth and development. When we avoid adversity and cling to comfort, we lose the edge to maintain the resilience needed to achieve levels of success each day. In speaking about resilience, the Mayo Clinic staff states, *"Resilience* won't *make your problems go away. But resilience can give you the ability to see past them, find enjoyment in life and handle stress better."*[xviii] Resilience is the ability to continue to function with a high degree of normalcy while experiencing adversity, trauma, tragedy, or stress. A prize-fighter would say, *"You roll with the punches."* The scriptures teach us to be content no matter what we are going through, to even become joyful through our difficulties.

If you are reading this now, I can conclude with a one hundred percent degree of certainty that so far, none of your troubling circumstances have killed you! In Major League Baseball, that would be batting one thousand percent and earn you a multi-million-dollar contract. However most people totally ignore such a solid track record and choose rather to stress, fear, and become inert with nearly every incoming adversity.

Children are not born with fears and inhibitions other than loud noises and falling. They would crawl into traffic and stroll through the mall naked and think nothing of it. We teach them to fear immediately after birth by imposing our own fears and inhibitions on them. The first words most kids learn are "no" and "stop"—hearing them often from adults, they quickly conform to a world gripped with fear and negativity.

The Solution Focused coach through empowerment questions, stimulates emotional intelligence.

In Daniel Goleman's work related to emotional intelligence, we get an understanding of how relentlessness and emotional intelligence connect with each other.

Goleman states,

"Motive and emotion share the same Latin root motere, 'to move.' Emotions are literally what move us to pursue our goals; they fuel our motivations, and our motives in turn drive our perceptions and shape our actions. Great work starts with great feeling."[xix]

Life coaches help clients to enhance their resilience levels; the resilient emotionally intelligent client greatly increases the likelihood of achieving the goals of coaching. Controlled, directed emotions are what motivate the client toward achieving goals.

The Solution Focused life coach uses empowering questions to draw out of the client positive emotions related to achievement and living the dream. This vicarious experience nourishes emotional intelligence, bolsters enthusiasm, and fortifies resilience. As clients continue to visualize themselves achieving their goals while actively pursuing them; it creates a double stimulating impact not easily denied.

The following list summarizes results from a study by Coert Visser, Ph.D. titled "Testing the Association between Solution-Focused Coaching and Client Perceived Coaching Outcomes" The study highlights 14 Solution Focused Coaching behaviors contributing to client satisfaction and goal attainment.

The coach focused on topics that I found useful to talk about *(client topic choice)*

After asking about my views, the coach accepted what I had said *(client perspective acknowledgement)*

The coach encouraged me to describe how I wanted my situation to become *(desired situation description)*

The coach encouraged me to describe what I wanted to be able to do differently *(positive future behavior description)*

The coach accepted and acknowledged my goal(s) *(client goal acceptance)*

The coach used the same words as I had used *(language matching)*

The coach gave me positive feedback (complimented me on what I had done well) *(positive behavior feedback)*

The coach checked several times whether our conversation was useful to me (*client usefulness check*)

The coach asked questions about what I had already done that had worked well (*exploration of what worked*)

The coach responded with understanding to what I said (*coach understanding and comprehension*)

The coach explained that what I said and did was normal (*normalizing*)

The coach subtly implied that my situation would become better (*positive expectation expression*)

The coach encouraged me to choose which step(s) forward I would like to take (*client chosen action*)

The coach let me decide whether the coaching should be continued or terminated (*client continuation choice*)

Example of Coaching Questions
Discovery Questions

- What changes in your life would you like to make?

- What could you change to make the situation more positive?

- What do you want to have success with first?

- What is the most important thing for you to accomplish right now?

Empowerment Questions

➤ What will reaching your goal look like?

➤ Will you list for me the things you know that are supporting your reaching this goal?

➤ Describe how good you really want to feel right now.

➤ Let's say you have reached your dreams, what new possibilities does this attainment bring?

➤ What are the most powerful two or three thoughts you could have related to this issue?

➤ What would you like to do differently than you are doing right now?

➤ Where is it you would really like to be?

➤ What are your life goals?

> If I were to ask you to sell this idea to me, how would you start?

> Can you think of a time when you believed you would have an absolutely victorious outcome in a situation; and what caused that belief?

> How good do you really want to feel right now?

> What would you like to see happen?

> If money was not an issue, what would you like to be doing right now?

> Has there ever been a time when you were successfully pursuing this goal and, what was it like?

> What are 3 or 4 things that absolutely motivate you and cause you to really want to do this?

> How would you describe how it will feel once you have achieved this?

> What things will be different once you achieve this dream or goal?

➢ How would you explain what your life would be like when you accomplish this?

➢ What will be the reaction of others who know you well once you accomplish this?

➢ How big would your dream be if there were a 100% chance of achieving it?

➢ How does a person reaching his/her greatest dream act?

➢ What is the best attitude you could have to bring about success as we work on these goals?

➢ Can you think of a time when you believed you would have a certain victory in a situation or were at the peak level of confidence and what caused that?

Solution Questions

• You won a free two-week trip to Hawaii leaving tomorrow; what steps would you take relative to home, business, and personal affairs to be free enough to go?

• What have you done in the past to deal with things like this?

- Has there ever been a time when you were successfully pursuing this, what caused you to do so?

- What steps are necessary to get your desired outcome?

- How could you make this turn out better?

- What are your plans to achieve your goals?

- What have you tried that has brought some successes?

- What needs to happen to get these plans going?

- What one thing could you do right now to make the biggest difference related to this?

- What would you like to leave here and be able to do right away?

- What things do you think you need to do to be able to achieve this?

- What do you believe you could do to turn this around immediately?

- Have you come up with any ideas to help with this concern?

- How can you restate this problem as a solution?

- What ideas would you have if everything you loved depended on you solving this issue?

- Tell me some things that could help turn this around?

- How do you think you can accomplish the things you want to accomplish?

- Can you list some things that may change this situation?

- What can you do to positively influence this?

Chapter 9
Now, Just Do it

Bill Bowerman was one of the greatest coaches to ever live. He coached many great track athletes, not the least of those was the great Steve Prefontaine, who was at his peak when an accident took his life on May 30, 1975. Steve was among the first athletes to wear Coach Bowerman's personally created track shoe which later launched the Blue Ribbon Company now known as NIKE whose slogan is "Just Do It"[xx]

I share a personal and special bond with Steve Prefontaine whose career and tragic death I remember as it were yesterday. Each year as I watch the Track and Field event at Eugene, Oregon named in his honor, I am reminded that he and I were born on the exact same day; January 25, 1951.

I was an athlete but not with the abilities "Pre" as he was affectionately called, was born with. Yet I have lived on, and he died at age 24. Forgive me for the somewhat morbid approach to making this point; but as a coach you've got to just do it! Of course I could go on and on about living in the moment as tomorrow is not promised to us, but I choose to make this point in this way. Bowerman also said, *"Believe in the power of the run."*[xxi]

Now I know he was referring to the literal running of the race, so let me offer you a related quote of my own. *"Aptitude is a great measuring standard, but it can only predict potential, effort reveals it."* There is no way to test what you have learned and no way to improve as a life coach unless you just do it. Every time I use the old hound dog story somebody makes a decision to just to it, so here goes.

There was an old man sitting on a ragged porch with his floppy eared hound dog. Periodically the dog would belt out a loud agonizing howl that could be heard for blocks. Soon appears a man walking along past the house just in time to hear what became famously known, during the O.J. Simpson trial, as a "plaintiff wale."

So the man asked sir, "what is wrong with that dog," to which the old man said," oh he's just lying on a nail that's sticking up through the floor". The pedestrian responded, "Why doesn't he move?" The old man said, "cause it ain't hurting bad enough".

Sometimes it's just hurting bad enough to complain about, but not to act upon. There is a phenomenon involving people talking about doing something so much they feel as though they have actually done it already. At some point the coach has got to just do it.

Of course you are going to meet with difficulties and challenges you will have to deal with on the fly. But nothing can ever take the place of real live experience. The sooner you get out of the classroom and into the greatly rewarding work of life coaching the sooner you will grow as a coach. Next, I'd like to offer some aid in dealing with some inevitable circumstances.

Coaching clients through difficulties

Sometimes teachers and advocates go to great extremes to drive home the importance of a position or stance. I, along with others have done this related to Life Coaching verses Therapy. The point we make and will continue to make is that a client who has or should have had a diagnosis should see a therapist not a life coach or perhaps both and not one who, as in my case, happens to be both. I will only serve as coach or therapist to a client, not both. Sometimes in our zeal as coaches we give the impression that a coach should never perform the role of a therapist during life coaching. I don't believe that.

When a coaching client is going through difficulties, and comes to a session uncharacteristically depressed, or dealing with an unexpected issue, I don't think he or she should be kicked out of the session and sent down the street to Dr. Feel Good. I see nothing wrong with using active listening skills and Rational Emotive or Cognitive Behavioral type coaching questions to challenge faulty, erroneous beliefs, which may be caging the client within a "poor me" mental prison.

The active listening may reveal client beliefs that are not rational. A simple question like, *"What are you really telling yourself about the problem,* may be enough to trigger more rational thinking and shake him or her back to reality. Remember these clients have only been unexpectedly hit with something troubling, they are not psychotherapy patients.

Are you sure you want my help?
Coaches need to know that there are clients who come for

coaching who really don't want help. One of the most freeing revelations I have come to in over 40 years in ministry is that Jesus himself never continued to try to help anybody who did not want help. Nothing is more frustrating and less rewarding than trying to help people who really don't want it. The only reward coming with that is a feeling of failure and incompetence.

This is true in every helping profession; and until the professional recognizes this when it is present, the best efforts only produce more and more frustration. There are various indicators of client resistance. Life coaches and therapists experience a level of resistance that is very contradictory and requires a keen since of awareness to identify. What makes this resistance difficult to detect is that one would suppose anyone coming to coaching really wants help to achieve certain things; not true.

As Jesus discovered, there are clients unwilling to pay the price involved with dream building, goal attainment or human growth and development. There are certain therapeutic benefits that occur for people who simply talk about a problem, goal, or dream. Again the psychological phenomenon transpires and gives the client the same sensation that a dream is accomplished, by simply talking about it a lot.

Life coaching is much more than just talking about what one would like to do. It is strategizing and working on the planned strategy. In every helping profession one encounters those who are content with talking and talking and talking and talking. They are not only talking to the coach, but to everyone else who will listen. They are speaking about anything from a light problem to a very large dream they would like to complete in their life someday. Any discussion of plans or strategies is welcomed, but there is no intention at all of doing them.

For one thing, if they did them and the problem was solved, or the dream was realized then they could no longer talk about it as a future event, which would absolutely ruin things. This is a form of client resistance not easily detected; but I assure you, those people don't really want help. Their self-esteem levels require psychotherapy, and you are a life coach. Your job is to take people who are achieving some level of success, wanting to do more, or become better and help them to do so.

On the other hand many of your clients will come to you because they have been slowed down or stuck due to some difficulties. These clients really do want help and there are ways to use Solution Focused Coaching to help them. There is nothing wrong with the coach taking on the form of a cheerleader and motivating through empowerment, praise, and truth.

If you are among the coaching purest and insist upon only using powerful questions in your sessions try this one. Instead of saying *"It's not what happens in life it's how you take it!"*[xxii] Curve Denis Waitley's exclamation point into a question mark and ask, what do you think the statement *"it's not what happens in life its how you take it"* means? Either way this refuting of irrational thinking may just lead to the use of more client empowering statements, Oops, I mean questions.

Coach for Intrinsic reasons first, then for money

The great New York Knickerbocker and U.S. Senator from New Jersey, Bill Bradley once said, *"Ambition is the path to success. Persistence is the vehicle you arrive in."*[xxiii] To paraphrase the Philosopher Epictetus *"Circumstances never make or break a person they merely reveal what is inside the person."* Because of my background in athletics and my life calling of bringing out the best in people, I cannot escape the coaching side of me motivating people, by holding them accountable to do things in excellence.

I refuse to allow my clients to escape the quest toward fulfilling the reasons they were placed on this earth in the first place. I have to admit, periodically I get a little preachy as a coach and fall into the Knute Rockne, Jim Valvano, go, go, get um, get um, rah, rah mode and my clients seem to benefit from it; they appreciate it. I am still a firm believer that coaches should talk 20% and client experts 80% of the coaching session. I strive hard not to violate this and see it as an early measure of successful coaching.

I consider the best of my work to have been performed with people who may not have achieved a great deal in life, had I not asked them certain coaching questions. I've asked many people questions like, *"When you go to sleep so you dream or do you "rise up" to live your dreams each day? If you could get paid very well to do what you really like to do what would it be? Will you describe for me; what the best day of your life looks like?"* These questions start us on a discovery mission to find what the client feels his/her real purpose in life is. Not long after that, questions inquiring as to what's preventing the pursuit of this or where do we start to chase this, lead to the enthusiastic establishment of goals, steps, and objectives.

I can't emphasis enough that the best way to ensure that you will never reach your goals is to not have any. The first step toward reaching a goal is to have one. We have known for some time now that upwards of 90 percent of America's population has no written life goals. Can you imagine the difference in the so-called average person's life to have a life coach facilitate the writing of life goals? And what if this was followed by the surfacing of objectives and steps to reach those goals? Now all that is left is a periodic coaching session for motivation, empowerment, and accountability. Sound simple? It really is.

There is one common theme related to those I have coached who were interested in achieving higher success levels. I generally ask a certain powerful question to facilitate large possibility thinking. I ask it of children in nearly every beginning session; and I ask it of adults early as well. I usually ask some form of the question, *"what would you be doing if there were no limits placed upon you?"* Or I may ask, "how large would your dream be if you know for certain you would reach it?" What separates adults from children is how they view life. Children live from moment to moment and seldom see disappointments as lethal to any future endeavors.

After an initial over-the-top response, kids quickly move on to the next challenge. Adults often mope around telling themselves things that could not be further from the truth and end up destroying what makes us all equal time. Time is the great equalizer as we all have the same 24 hours per day, 168 each week within which to rise up early and chase our dreams all day long.

I consider it my calling or my specialty to help people who may be selling themselves a bit short, reveal the golden nugget buried inside and challenge them to live up to it. A great sculpture artist creating beautiful granite sculptures, always walked around the huge mass of granite for hours, sometimes days before striking away the first chip. When asked why, his response in essence was that he had to get a solid mental image of the masterpiece that was inside the granite before beginning to chip away everything else.

I believe that greatness in some field of endeavor is inside us all. A life coach, who specializes in helping people reach their greatest dreams, will help clients to clearly see the potential inside and set out to chip away whatever is hindering them from achieving their dream. The goals may then take on dealing with things like a lack of education, low self-esteem, discipline, organization and more.

When someone has a dream and is determined to

reach it, individual obstacles become much clearer. These obstacles become coaching focal points and steppingstones toward the fruition of the dream.

I met a person who in the minds of many had already lived the best years of her life. In her early 50s, I asked her what her greatest dream was. She said I want to be a lawyer. This lady was a single divorcee who loved kids. She loved them so much that she adopted four, fostered several and had two grown children of her own. Though not at all poor in spirit, she would be classified poor by United States government criteria.

This story is still being created, but at this time she has earned a bachelor's degree, master's degree and is still doing all the wonderful things she does for children and is one of the best mothers I have ever met. Whether she keeps pursuing her dream or even if it changes, she has clearly taken a shot for the moon and so far, landed on a star.

The people born with a silver spoon in their mouth are not the only ones with great potential. That is why the obstacles overcome are a much better barometer than a person's achievements. Everyone is excited to coach the executive who is very motivated and very able to pay. I know; *"somebody's got to do it."* I agree; this is not a slight, in any way. However the point here is that some people face more difficult challenges than others and this is no indication of their potential; they have golden nuggets inside too!

I urge you to do some pro-bono work, have a sliding scale or start community group coaching sessions with nominal fees, to help people reach their greatest dreams. We all owe a debt to society for the air we breathe, and resources used; this would be a great way to give some of it back. The experience you gain and the contribution to enhancing lives will be immeasurable. You will not have to look far for clients willing to submit themselves to a life coach for little or no fee, for you to gain experience.

Because the idea of life coaching has almost reached fad level, people are very proud to boast about having their own life, or business coach. While I would never encourage you to sell yourself too cheaply, the benefit gained through experience is financially immeasurable. So if you feel you should start now to charge large amounts of money or feel you should gain more experience in Solution Focused Coaching that matters little. What is important is that you do not sit on this and do like the hound dog I spoke about earlier. You are more than ready, now; just Do it!

Conclusion

The goal for this book was for it to be written in a simple and easily understood style encouraging the practical use of the content. The stories, illustrations and metaphors used are for the purpose of aiding to serve that end.

The helping profession research world is cluttered with too many attempts to impress other researchers, and too few with simply applied practical instructions, related to using that valuable research.

While critical thinking and academia have a solid responsibility and helps hold us accountability to best practices, it is very close to becoming a god unto itself, totally separate from the clinical support use it should serve.

Some of the best research information never makes it into the hands of most dedicated practitioners; and when it does it is often too technical, boring and clinician unfriendly, to serve its purpose. It seems that some of the best information is written to impress a research-based constituency, which requires too much wading through mumbo jumbo to get to something useful for quick application and practice.

Serious practitioners also need to lighten up a bit, rekindle our learning mode and through relaxation, reduce the high stress levels commensurate with so many helping professions. Life coaches, especially those willing to work with clients not socio-economically elite and practitioners having a compassionate heart, are going to experience times of intense desire to see clients reach their dreams, though they have been dealt a bowl of lemons.

Our histories are filled with people who were dealt lemons and made lemonade with them; people like a blind and deaf Helen Keller, whose autobiography has been translated into more than 50 languages, a crippled Wilma Rudolph, 4-time Olympic goal medalist and Quadriplegic Kyle Maynard, wrestling champion, and a stuttering James Earl Jones, Actor extraordinaire. There are too many more with great potential that are not making it at all. Life coaches with big hearts and a strong sense of mission can help decrease that failure number significantly.

This book was written with the purpose of putting many more boots on the ground, equipped with the most effective life coaching techniques currently available. I am offering coaches a way of viewing Solution Focused Coaching that will make its practice accessible, appealing, and more likely to be used, leading to greater coaching success. I trust you will have found it to be informative, refreshing, and practical enough to use as a reference or at least to be referred to periodically. It will serve well to sharpen your solution focused skills for continued effectiveness.

As a coach I would like to know that you did not go to your grave with your music still in you. That you don't go to bed each night perhaps to dream; but you instead wake up to live your dreams every day.

I insist that you know earning large sums of money as a coach is only an extrinsic motivator and that the opportunity to coach a child or adult to reach his or her greatest dream is an intrinsic motivator. Intrinsic motivators endure the tests of time, circumstances, obstacles, and frustrations.

Intrinsic motivation is what offers the best reply to our 35th President John F. Kennedy's heartfelt plea to Americans; *"Ask not what your country can do for you, ask what you can do for your country."* I hope that you make tons of money as a life coach. But I hope even more that you can use your life coaching skills to aid in improving the lives of many Americans who will improve the lives of many thousands more.

That is why this book was written. So coach, here's an empowerment question for you; *"Given your tremendous potential to help change a life for the positive, what will be your next steps toward changing your world? I'm just asking!*

Definitions, Designations and Descriptions

Active listening: Using certain listening skills that help the client to reach deep inside to share valuable information needed to set and reach client goals and objectives.

Awfulizing: The mental and verbal process of assigning irrational negative beliefs to an issue, problem, or circumstance.

Catastrophic prediction: An inward and often expressed belief that an issue or situation is or will become a disaster.

Coachee/Client: The person being coached considered in Coaching to be the expert.

Coaching: The use of powerful and insightful questions to bring to the surface, deeply concealed dreams, potential and life development goals; then holding the coachee responsible for strategies, to chase, and seize them all.

Coaching focal points (CFP): The Client's and coach's agreed goals to be coached.

Cocooning: The process of withdrawing emotionally to prepare for further growth and development.

Discovery questions: Coaching questions used to determine coaching focal points, strengths, resources, and supports.

Emotional Intelligence: The level of which a person responds emotionally to situations and circumstances, affecting success and achievement.

Empowerment questions: Question designed to offer support and endorsement to encourage, motivate and engage client in more goal achieving action.

Exceptions: Pinpointed occasions when the client's problem or reason for seeking coaching is not in effect or at issue. These are seen as opportunities to forward progressive action by purposely doing more of whatever causes that to occur.

Mentoring: Differs from coaching in that mentoring involves the mentor often lecturing and being an example for the mentee who is in some way, trying to duplicate some aspect of the mentor.

Miracle question: A question designed to cause the client to describe the scene after a miracle took place related to their dream, desire, or reason for seeking coaching.

Person Centered Therapy: A counseling approach espoused by Carl Rogers involving the facilitation of an atmosphere conducive to the client bringing from within him or herself the solution to his/her own problems.

Powerful questions: Questions usually open ended promoting deep thought, resulting in the client's voicing of strategies, solutions, dreams, ideas, and plans related to problem solving and goal attainment.

Psychotherapist: A trained professional who diagnosis and treats mental illness.

Rational Emotive Therapy (RET): A type of Psychotherapy related to Albert Ellis summed up by saying "it is not what happens in life, but how you accept what happens in life that determines its effect.

Reframing: To offer an alternate view of things, usually with a positive, productive spin empowering the client.

Scaling questions: Questions asked to determine a client's perceived status level related to coaching focal points and what can be done to move to a higher level on the positive side up the scale.

Self-awareness: A client's discovery and assessment of who he or she is; focused less on negatives and more on hidden abilities, positive character traits and helping forces; which will assist in the attainment of goals objectives and dreams.

Solution Focused Therapy: A Psychotherapy approach developed by Steve de Shazar and Insoo Kim Berg in 1982 focusing on solutions not problems.

Solution questions: Question to the client attempting to solicit solutions from within the client relative to coaching focal points.

Visualization: To vicariously envision oneself actually living the dream, activity, condition, or state sought through coaching.

References

Goleman, D. (2006). *Working with Emotional Intelligence*: Bantam Dell, New York, NY.

O'Connell, B. Palmer, S. Williams, H. (2012). *Solution Focused Coaching in Practice*: Routledge, New York, NY.

Tracy, B. Fraser, C. (2005). *Turbo Coach*: American Management Association, New York, NY.

Waitley, D. (1984). *The Psychology of Winning:* Berkley Publishing Corporation New York, NY.

Williams, P. Menendez, D. (2007). *Becoming A Professional Life Coach.* W.W. Norton & Co. New York, NY.

Web Sites

www.YesICan1.com

www.solutionfocused.net/solutionfocusedtherapy.html

http://www.brainyquote.com/quotes/authors/r/ralph_waldo_emerson_4.html

http://www.brainyquote.com/qoutes/authors/y/yogi_berra.htm/

http://www.psychologytoday.com/blog/in-therapy/201001/ cool-intervention-10-the-miracle-question

http://www.huffingtonpost.com/2013/03/04/jimmy-v-speech-video-valvano-espy_n_2806888.html

http://www.butterflyschool.org/new/meta.html

http://sports.espn.go.com/mlb/news/story?id=4939095

http://www.brainyquote.com/quotes/authors/e/emmitt_smith.html

http://www.marvlevy.net/

http://www.enotes.com/shakespeare-quotes/thine-own-self-true

http://www.gottmanblog.com/2012/12/the-positive-perspective-dr-gottmans.html

http://www.frontiernet.net/~docbob/shuttle.htm

http://www.coachwooden.com/index2.html

http://www.mayoclinic.org/healthy-living/adult-health/in-depth/resilience/art-20046311

http://nikeinc.com/pages/history-heritage

Endnotes

[i] www.**solutionfocused**.net/**solutionfocusedtherapy**.html

[ii] http://www.brainyquote.com/quotes/authors/r/ralph_waldo_emerson_4.html

[iii] http://www.brainyquote.com/qoutes/authors/y/yogi_berra.htm/

[iv] http://www.psychologytoday.com/blog/in-therapy/201001/cool-intervention-10-the-miracle-question

[v] http://www.huffingtonpost.com/2013/03/04/jimmy-v-speech-video-valvano-espy_n_2806888.html

[vi] New International Bible (1986)

[vii] http://www.butterflyschool.org/new/meta.html

[viii] http://sports.espn.go.com/mlb/news/story?id=4939095

[ix] New International Bible (1986)

[x] http://www.brainyquote.com/quotes/authors/e/emmitt_smith.html

[xi] Goleman, D. (2006). *Working with Emotional Intelligence.* New York, NY: Bantam Dell

[xii] http://www.marvlevy.net/

[xiii] http://www.enotes.com/shakespeare-quotes/thine-own-self-true

[xiv] New International Bible (1986)

[xv] http://www.gottmanblog.com/2012/12/the-positive-perspective-

dr-gottmans.html

[xvi]http://www.frontiernet.net/~docbob/shuttle.htm

[xvii]http://www.coachwooden.com/index2.html

[xviii]http://www.mayoclinic.org/healthy-living/adult-health/in-depth/resilience/art-20046311

[xix]Goleman, D. (2006). *Working with Emotional Intelligence.* New York, NY: Bantam Dell

[xx]http://nikeinc.com/pages/history-heritage

[xxi]http://nicerunningday.tumblr.com/post/27210765062/believe-in-the-power-of-the-run

[xxii]Waitley, D. (2005). The Psychology of Winning. Made for Success, Inc.

[xxiii] http://www.biography.com/people/bill-bradley-9223478

www.ingramcontent.com/pod-product-compliance
Lightning Source LLC
Chambersburg PA
CBHW040148160726
48006CB00014B/1659